First published in the UK in 2002 by Circle Books
Circle Books
83/84 George Street
Richmond
Surrey TW9 1HE
Phone: 020 8332 2709

© British Sub-Aqua Club
Telford's Quay, South Pier Road
Ellesmere Port
Cheshire CH65 4FL
Phone: 0151 350 6200

Author
Deric Ellerby

Editor
Paul Critcher

Art Editor
Alistair Cook

Illustrations: Ian Legge
Source illustrations: Daphne Ellerby

Printing
Compass Press Limited
100-104 Upper Richmond Road
London SW15 2SP
Phone: 020 8780 7000

ISBN: 0-9538919-2-5

The Diving Manual

An introduction to scuba diving

Foreword

For 50 years the British Sub-Aqua Club has been at the forefront of recreational diving. In that time many divers, including myself, have benefited from its excellent training. I am delighted to introduce this new manual, which has been specifically produced for beginners. I feel sure it will stimulate and inform all newcomers to the fascinating sport of scuba diving. Qualifying as a diver is a tremendously rewarding experience and I am certain this book will encourage many more people to discover the joys of the underwater world.

HRH Prince Charles

Table of contents

Table of contents

Breaking the surface chapter three

Deeper in knowledge chapter four

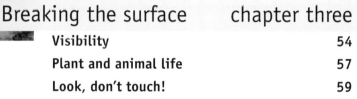

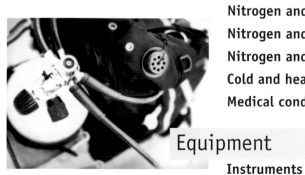

Equipment chapter five

Table of contents

More diving skills   chapter six

A different world   chapter seven

What next? chapter eight

Introduction

Most people's experience of the oceans is limited to a walk on the beach or perhaps a brief splash in the sea during the summer, but for the diver the realm beneath the oceans is a beautiful world which is endlessly fascinating. For those unfamiliar with the joys of diving, this book aims to provide pertinent information and will act as the starting point for your underwater adventure.

Introduction
The wonder of diving

Diving beneath the surface of the oceans and seas occurs for a variety of reasons, including scientific, military and commercial, but by far the greatest number of people who dive do so for pleasure.

For many, the chance to enter a 'new world' in which weightlessness, space and freedom of movement combine to offer a wholly different experience from our everyday world is motivation enough to join the ranks of divers throughout the world. However, once a basic level of training has been completed, more opportunities to explore and appreciate our oceans are unleashed. The oceans cover seven tenths of our world, and the scope for underwater activities is similarly wide. The underwater world is one of remarkable contrasts of colour and topography, with a diverse array of fish, plants and animals, all of which are in stark contrast to our usual earthbound surroundings. Aquatic animals range in size and type, from small organisms such as plankton, to the largest of the world's mammals, the blue whale.

The stunning vistas below the seas are not just pretty to look at, but provide the photographer and videographer with a different sphere in which to work, allowing them to make use of shadow and light in a whole new genre.

History and anthropology also lure many divers into the water – the chance to dive on wrecks, which now play host to schools of fish and colourful marine life, or the search for lost civilisations. Underwater archaeology is an exacting yet rewarding pursuit.

Whatever your interest in the marine environment, the waters of our blue planet offer the chance of limitless choice and enjoyment.

Today, the underwater world can be accessed at many different levels, varying from simple underwater tourism to a whole variety of professional activities. For most commercial activities it is usually the specific skills and knowledge of the profession that are crucial, diving being merely a transport activity. Similarly, in the recreational field, diving can also be seen as a mode of transport enabling many leisure activities from our normal world to be pursued underwater. The level of these diving activities can range from a basic guided underwater tour to a high-tech challenge of our current underwater limits. Whatever the ultimate diving goal, there has to be a beginning, and the purpose of this book is to provide useful information to the new diver. Whether your aim is simply to be a diving tourist or to seek out the submarine equivalents of Himalayan ascents, the underwater world awaits.

The simplest beginning to scuba diving is just to sample the underwater world under the careful control of an experienced guide/instructor. This can be achieved in a variety of situations, ranging from a local swimming pool to a dive at an exotic holiday destination. This first underwater experience may be provided by a diving club or a diving school. A choice preferred by many is to undertake an entry-level diver training course, again provided by either a club or a school. This, too, can take place locally or while away on holiday, with a typical course lasting some four or five days and normally including four or five dives.

Divers can enjoy the wonders of the underwater world

Non-swimmers

A diving instructor takes two students for a lesson

Non-swimmers

When recreational diving began, it was seen very much as the province of fit young men and the training was rather military in nature, a diver was something of a pioneer and equipment was often home-made. Today, access to diving has totally changed. Thanks to modern equipment and training techniques, diving is available to virtually everyone of normal fitness, from people in their early teens to octogenarians. There is often a belief that diving is only for the strongest of swimmers, but nothing could be further from the truth – the swimming techniques used for unaided movement at the surface and the consequent breath-control patterns are far removed from the relaxed fin strokes and natural breathing of a competent diver. While most diver-training agencies do require a student to have a basic swimming ability, the key to success as a diver is to be relaxed in the water and comfortable with the equipment.

Indeed, there are many previous non-swimmers who have become proficient divers and swimmers through the water confidence they have gained from the use of fins, dive mask and snorkel. Surface swimming is a complex process that combines three basic features – confidence, breathing and movement. In learning to swim, movement is often perceived as the key skill to learn, but it is breathing and water confidence that are crucial. Non-swimmers often lack confidence while in the water, because they have not been able to master the breathing element. The provision of an air supply using either scuba (Self-Contained Underwater Breathing Apparatus) or even a simple snorkel tube solves the breathing problem, allowing the non-swimmer to gain water confidence. With water confidence the rest is easy. The key requirement is a desire to visit the underwater world: so what are you waiting for?

Students learn some theory

Practising skills in a swimming pool

An open-water dive

Learning to dive

Born as land creatures, we obviously need some extra support to enable us to explore the underwater world safely and happily. Support comes partly from the equipment we use and partly from the extra skills and knowledge we need to acquire. This immediately raises two questions: what equipment is needed and what degree of skill and knowledge is appropriate. The answers are extremely variable, depending totally on the kind of diving envisaged.

Underwater tourism

At the simplest level, diving can be enjoyed simply as an underwater tourist. The diving instructor takes total responsibility for the equipment of the student, ensuring it is fit for the planned dive, and all that is required of the user is to wear it and breathe from it. Similarly, the level of skill and knowledge required is also very basic, often being delivered as an extended briefing just before the dive. Elementary use of the equipment is demonstrated along with balancing pressure on the ears and recommended breathing rhythm. Armed with this very basic education and escorted on a one-to-one basis by the instructor, the tourist can start to explore the underwater world. The dives will be limited, lasting between ten and 15 minutes and to a maximum depth of 5–6m (metres). However, the first fin strokes can be made. These shallow depths are often home to an abundance of life forms, especially if the dives are made on reefs.

Entry-level training

Such experiences usually whet the appetite for repeat dives and here a further decision must be taken. It is possible to continue as a perpetual underwater tourist, but such intensive support from the instructor is very demanding on the resources of a dive centre and this will have to be reflected in the charges it makes. Furthermore, the challenge of more adventurous dives will be tempting you to visit places which require longer underwater times and descents to greater depths. Naturally, this also means a higher level of skill and knowledge will be required. Also, as such diving usually occurs in groups organised by a club or school, there is a greater need for self-responsibility. The simple answer to these needs is a progressive system of education which matches the students' needs. Such training is usually offered as an entry-level course typically taking either a few days of fairly intensive training or lasting some weeks, occupying an evening each week. Whichever option, the course should provide the student with the necessary skills and knowledge to safely enjoy diving to a maximum of 20m in water conditions matching those where the course was taken. The entry-level diver certification you gain after completing such a course will normally be recognised by other responsible dive centres when you travel to other dive sites, avoiding the need for repeat certification. Of course, if some years have passed since such training has taken place and there is no evidence of regular and recent dive experience, some refresher training may be advisable.

Signalling to the support team on the boat that all is 'okay'

A student learns how to set up her kit

Using the buddy system during an open-water dive

Knowledge

What knowledge is provided at this entry level? The prospective diver will require an elementary understanding of the equipment and its use, an understanding of the physical and physiological effects of being underwater in these depths, and some awareness of the underwater environment. You will also want some knowledge of the various activities that can be pursued underwater. This book is designed to provide you, the student, with some background to the knowledge you gain from your instructor and act as your reference source as an entry-level diver.

While most knowledge will be best absorbed in a classroom environment, practical skills are generally water-based. Most skills will be introduced to the student in calm, sheltered conditions, often in a swimming pool. You will learn how to handle mask, fins and the scuba unit, and how to enter and exit the water as a fully equipped diver. One of the most important yet exciting skills is the achievement of neutral buoyancy, enabling you to truly feel weightless in the water.

Progression

As your skills and knowledge develop, you will be taken on the first of your open-water dives. These dives will be carefully chosen to suit your capabilities and to help you learn techniques such as buddy diving, ascent and descent and simple navigation. You will gradually appreciate the various marine life forms in all their colour, diversity and camouflage. Skills previously learned in your sheltered-water lessons will be further developed and polished and by the time of your certification you will have mastered the basics of scuba diving. You should be capable of being a competent dive buddy (of which, more later) in the depth zone and waters you have experienced, and have a foundation of knowledge and skill to commence your exploration of the undersea realm. □

Chapter one

Adapting to the underwater world

As land creatures, our bodies are adapted to a life surrounded by the atmosphere and pinned to the earth's surface by the force of gravity. Even as swimmers we are restricted to the water's surface and need exposure to the atmosphere to continue to breathe. Scuba (Self-Contained Underwater Breathing Apparatus) equipment changes all that – the diver has a breathing supply and can descend to explore the underwater world. In descending, the important physical effects of diving rapidly become apparent...

Adapting
To the underwater world

At sea level the 250,000m-deep layer of atmosphere exerts a pressure equal to 1 bar

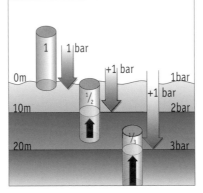

As pressure increases with depth, air is compressed and takes up less space

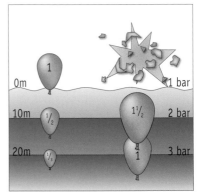

Pressure decreases on ascent, causing the compressed air inside a balloon filled at depth to expand

Pressure

At the surface of the earth we experience the pressure created by the 250,000m-deep layer of air that makes up the atmosphere. At sea level the weight of this layer is equal to 1kg (kilogram) pressing on every square centimetre of surface. As you experience this pressure all your life, your body is naturally adapted to it and you experience no notable sensation. In diving, it is customary to refer to the sea level atmospheric pressure as '1 bar'. Water is much denser than air and as you descend through it, the pressure it exerts on your body increases. As most parts of your body have a similar density to water, these parts suffer no adverse effects and, indeed, provide no sensation of pressure. The exceptions are the various cavities in the body which contain air, such as the lungs, middle ear and sinuses. The air in these cavities is exposed to an increased pressure, depending on the depth of the diver. To understand how this affects you and how to adapt to these effects, you need to understand what happens to gases such as those found in air when the pressure is increased.

Depth

A mere 10m depth of water creates the same pressure (1 bar) as the whole depth of the atmosphere. Starting from the zero pressure (0 bar) of space, we progress to 1-bar pressure at sea level and so have 2-bar pressure at a depth of 10m. Each additional 10m of depth adds another 1 bar of pressure. While water can be considered incompressible, this is not the case with gases. If a quantity of gas, such as the air in your lungs, is taken to a depth of 10m, where the pressure is double that at sea level (2 bar), it is squashed to occupy only half its surface volume. This relationship continues so that at 20m, with a pressure of 3 bar, its volume will reduce to one third. Were you to dive by simply holding your breath, the elasticity of your lungs could cope with this reduction in volume over quite a depth range. The diaphragm moves upwards into the chest cavity to compensate, often resulting in a flattering slim waistline! Of course, things revert to normal on return to the surface, as the pressure reduces and the air in your lungs expands to its original volume.

The scuba unit, comprised of an air cylinder, a regulator and a buoyancy compensator

A regulator allows the scuba diver to breathe on demand from a cylinder of compressed air

Breathing underwater

As a scuba diver, you will breathe underwater from your scuba unit. This provides air easily and comfortably through a mouthpiece whenever you try to breathe in, and allows you to breathe out equally easily. The air is supplied at the same pressure as the water surrounding you (ambient pressure), and you will automatically fill your lungs (and connecting airways) to their normal surface volume for the same inhalation effort. So, no slim waistline! This means that you experience no difficulty in continuing a normal breathing pattern appropriate to your underwater activity level (sedentary fish-watching, vigorous finning, and so on). It also brings us to the first conscious adaptation you must make. A normal human reaction is to hold one's breath whenever the face is wet, preventing a lot of coughing and spluttering when face washing. However, as a scuba diver you obviously have to overcome this reaction and keep breathing normally. This is particularly important whenever ascending through the water. The air in your lungs will have been breathed in at the pressure of the water surrounding you at the moment of inhalation. In ascending, the surrounding pressure will reduce

and the effect of this on a volume of gas is to allow it to expand. If this were to happen to the air contained in your lungs it would either stretch your lungs or the excess would have to be exhaled. Expanding your lungs in this manner is dangerous, and in extreme cases can cause severe damage or even death. The golden rule is 'Never hold your breath when breathing from a scuba unit'. Always adopt a normal breathing rhythm, being especially careful during any ascent.

The scuba unit

The scuba unit consists of an air cylinder, a regulator and a buoyancy compensator. The high-pressure cylinder enables the large volume of air needed for the dive to be compressed into a manageable space. It is mounted on the buoyancy compensator and worn on the diver's back. Commonly, cylinders with an internal volume of between 10 and 12 litres are used, pressurised to at least 200 bar. This is 200 times atmospheric pressure and effectively means that the volume of air of some 200 cylinders is squashed into one cylinder! Cylinders are made from steel or aluminium alloy.

Equalising

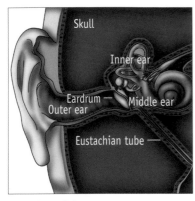

Physiology of the ear

Ears

Most people have experienced the sensation of pressure, and even pain, in the ear when simply swimming underwater. This is caused by the pressure of the water acting on the outside surface of the eardrum. The inside of the eardrum is exposed to the pressure of the air in the middle ear, which will usually be the same as the air at the surface. If no adaptation is made, the increasing pressure that comes with increasing depth would eventually cause the eardrum to rupture. To avoid this the scuba diver allows air from the mouth/nasal passage to pass through the Eustachian tube into the middle ear. As this air is at the same pressure as the surrounding water, the pressure on the eardrum is balanced and the problem removed. The clever trick, referred to as 'ear clearing' (or 'equalising') by divers, is persuading the air to pass through the Eustachian tube. This is normally closed, but can often be opened by a swallowing or a jaw-wriggling action. Failing these, breathing out against a pinched nose can raise the air pressure in the back of the throat sufficient to force some air up the Eustachian tube and balance the middle-ear pressure. It is important not to strain too hard with this manoeuvre. The best technique is to perform ear clearing as soon as any sensation of pressure is felt, and well before this develops into pain. Any pain is a symptom of damage. If successful ear clearing cannot be performed, you must reduce your depth and therefore the pressure before trying ear clearing again. Nose and throat infections often cause inflammation of the Eustachian tube, which may prevent ear clearing. In these circumstances diving should not be attempted.

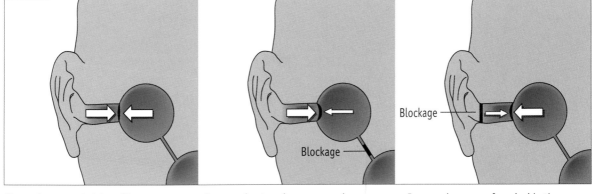

The ear in a normal state, with balanced pressure on the eardrum

Increased external pressure and a blocked Eustachian tube stretches the eardrum inwards

Increased pressure from inside the ear and a blocked outer ear stretches the eardrum outwards

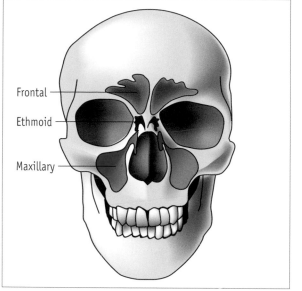

Sinuses are air spaces in the bone of the skull

A mask is a vital piece of a diver's equipment

Sinuses and other spaces

Sinuses are rigid spaces filled with air within the bone of the skull and are mostly connected and open to the upper nasal passages. Normally the air pressure within them will adjust automatically. However, it is possible that mucus or inflammation during nose and throat infections can block them – another reason for not diving until recovered. There are usually pockets of gas in the stomach and gut, but the responses of these gases to increases and decreases in pressure should not cause problems.

Seeing underwater

Our eyes have developed to operate normally when in contact with air. As water has different optical properties from air, direct contact with the eyes produces very blurred vision. To overcome this problem you need a diving mask, which will trap a pocket of air around the eyes and provide a window for you to look through.

As it is close to the eyes, it is important that this window is of tempered (safety) glass. The body of the mask needs to make a comfortable seal with the face and allow access for you to pinch your nose for ear clearing. The mask contains air, which will reduce in volume as you descend and this can cause the mask to squeeze the face and result in bruising (black eyes). The remedy is simple: diving masks also enclose the nose, allowing you to breathe out ambient-pressure air into the mask as you descend – no more bruising. On ascent, excess air will escape from the mask skirt automatically. As the water outside the mask will be colder than the body-temperature air inside, moisture will condense on the inside of the glass. Coating it with an anti-fogging product before diving can prevent condensation. Many divers use saliva instead, simply spitting on the inside of the glass, rubbing the saliva around and rinsing the mask in the sea immediately before diving. For those needing spectacles or contact lenses, masks with corrective lenses are also available.

Propulsion

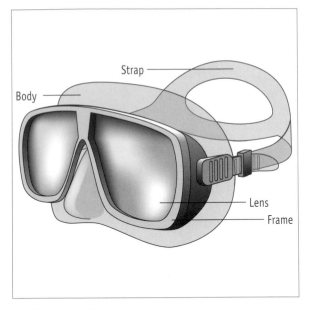

A typical scuba-diving mask

Fins: top, a full-shoe-style fin; bottom, a heel-strap-style fin

The mask

Frame – secures the body to the lens.
Strap – either a split or single strap, holding the mask against the face. Buckles allow the length of the strap to be adjusted.
Lens – scratch and shatter-resistant and usually made from tempered glass. Avoid plastic, which tends to scratch and fog more easily.
Body – usually made from a soft-rubber compound to form a waterproof seal against the diver's face. Non-allergenic silicone rubber is often used for the body of the mask as it maintains its flexibility over a wide temperature range and is very long-lasting. Translucent materials are popular because they allow light to enter the body of the mask.

Test a new mask for comfort and correct fit by putting it on your face without using the strap and inhaling. A correctly fitting mask will stay in place until you exhale through your nose. Choose a mask with a good angle of vision both vertically and horizontally. Avoid masks which have built-in snorkels.

Propulsion

Conventional swimming is neither effective nor appropriate when diving with scuba equipment. Instead, propulsion comes from fins fitted to the feet, leaving the hands free for equipment management and other tasks. The fin is made up of two main parts – the shoe and the blade. The shoe may fully enclose the heel, or just the front of the foot and have a heel-retaining strap. If you intend diving in warm water with bare feet or lightweight bootees or socks, a full-shoe-style may be comfortable. For colder water in which you will be wearing thick boots, the heel-strap-style will be more practical. Whichever style you use, it is important that you achieve a good fit, neither too tight so as to constrict or so slack that it causes chafing. The blade is usually of a harder material and may incorporate stiffening ridges, slots and other devices to enhance the propulsive effect. Heel straps should be easily adjustable and many come with quick-release features to assist removal. Many divers prefer to own rather than rent fins, in which case, for travel, the weight of the fins may be a consideration when buying them.

The buoyancy compensator

The buoyancy compensator (BC) – sometimes known as a buoyancy compensation device or BCD – serves two main functions. It acts as a harness, allowing you to wear the air cylinder on your back, and also allows you to introduce or release air from its chamber(s), thereby altering your overall buoyancy. The harness can vary from a simple waistcoat-style with an adjustable waist strap, to complex designs with adjustable shoulder, chest and waist straps. The waist strap frequently takes the form of, or is supplemented by, a Velcro-fastening cummerbund helping distribute the weight of the scuba unit more equally across the hips and providing added security and comfort. The cylinder is usually connected to the BC by a quick-release strap mechanism. Make sure that your BC is correct for your size and, while fitting securely, can be quickly jettisoned.

The BC will also have an air hose connecting it to the medium-pressure side of the regulator first stage. This provides a medium-pressure air supply from which to inflate the BC, thus increasing your buoyancy - referred to as a direct feed or power inflator. There will also be another hose allowing inflation by mouth, which is possible underwater but usually reserved for surface operation. This mouth inflation tube commonly incorporates the control valve for direct inflation and also for releasing air from the BC to decrease buoyancy. These manual controls provide fine buoyancy control, but there will also be an automatic pressure-relief valve to prevent accidental overpressurisation of the BC, and frequently this can also be manually operated. Such devices are often referred to as 'dump valves', as they allow a rapid dumping of air (and positive buoyancy).

The buoyancy compensator allows the diver to adjust his or her buoyancy

Protective clothing is worn in order to
maintain body heat

Wetsuits are popular when diving in warmer water

Drysuits are more appropriate for temperate and cold-water diving

Protective clothing

On most dives some form of protection other than a conventional swimsuit is appropriate. Probably the main reason for extra protection is to maintain body heat. Even in tropical waters the duration of a dive can be enough to cause discomfort brought on by cold, while in more temperate or polar climes the need for thermal protection is obvious. Although it is good dive practice to avoid unnecessary contact with marine life, some form of abrasion protection is also often wise. For these reasons a variety of protective clothing solutions have evolved, which are specifically manufactured for the diver.

You normally provide your body with thermal insulation by trapping a layer of air close to your skin. This air is warmed by body heat and, because air is a poor conductor of heat, gives you a stable thermal environment. If that layer of air is removed by wind, draught or deliberate ventilation, you are cooled, so windproof clothing helps keep you warm. Water is 25 times better at heat conduction than air, so you will cool much more rapidly when submerged. The flow of heat from your body will warm the water that immediately surrounds it; therefore, preventing it flowing away by some form of protective clothing will help reduce heat loss.

In tropical waters even a T-shirt can be sufficient thermal protection in the warm waters near the surface. For protection in deeper waters, thin Lycra suits can serve the dual purpose of abrasion and thermal protection, besides looking stylish on the right figure.

For improved heat retention, wetsuits tailored from foam neoprene – a synthetic rubber – are popular. The gas bubbles in the neoprene help make it a poor conductor of heat and the thin layer of water trapped inside a close-fitting suit is soon warmed to near body temperature. Suits of different thicknesses and style, often worn with hoods and gloves, can be chosen appropriate to the temperature of the waters being dived. For colder waters, drysuits with seals at the neck and wrists which keep the water away from the body can be worn. These drysuits instead trap a layer of air against the body, often using warm under-clothing, and so help maintain body temperature. □

Chapter two

Basic underwater skills

While scuba diving is by no means a difficult pursuit, there are some basic skills which need to be learned. These range from equipment checks to underwater communication and are essential for both a diver's safety and comfort. Learning these skills is an ongoing process and the key to improving your diving is practise, practise, practise. Eventually, you will find that performing buddy checks and mask clearing become second nature, while familiarisation with safety procedures should increase your confidence.

Basic underwater skills
Communication

'I am okay,' or 'Are you okay?' Used as both a question and a reply.

'Stop, stay where you are.' This signal is often followed by more signals explaining why.

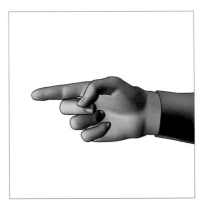

'You' or 'Me'. The diver points to himself or another diver, indicating the person referred to in the signal which follows.

Diving is an activity best shared with others, so an ability to communicate between divers is important. This is particularly so while you are learning – good instructor/student communication is vital. We use all of our senses to convey information and the ability to hear speech is of major importance in our day-to-day life. However, underwater with a diving regulator in your mouth, speech is not a realistic option. Instead, as soon as you start breathing from a regulator, divers communicate using an internationally recognised system of simple hand signals. Inevitably, local dialects creep in to augment such a system, so it is always wise when diving in a new locality, or with strangers, to check what signals are understood.

Divers use these signals to communicate between members of the group both underwater and at the surface. Some signalling is also necessary between divers in the water and their surface support, who are either in a boat or on the shore. In communicating these signals divers pose questions, provide responses and make statements, such as:

'Are you okay?'

'I am okay.'

'Go this way.'

'Descend' or 'Ascend.'

Make sure you have the attention of the diver you are signalling and that you give slow, clear signals within that person's field of vision.

'Go up,' or 'I am going up.' An instruction to ascend.

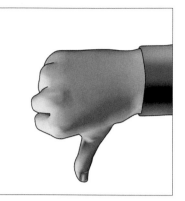

'Go down,' or 'I am going down.' An instruction to descend.

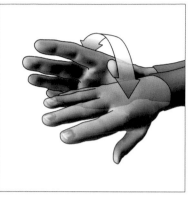

'Something is wrong.' This is not a sign of emergency, but an indication that all is not well.

'I am in distress.' Should you see this signal offer the distressed diver immediate help.

Distress at surface. 'Come and get me.' The signal demands immediate assistance for the signalling diver.

Okay at surface. 'I am okay.' Used to indicate to the surface support that all is well

'I am out of breath.' By moving his or her hands to and fro, your buddy indicates fatigue/breathlessness.

'I have no more air.' Move your outstretched hand back and forth horizontally from your throat.

'I am on reserve,' or 'I am on 50 bar,' used to indicate that the diver's air supply is low.

A diver signals that his air supply is low

Attaching a regulator and BC to a cylinder

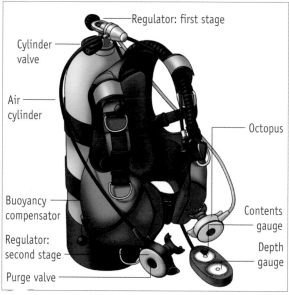

Regulator: first stage

Cylinder valve

Air cylinder

Octopus

Buoyancy compensator

Contents gauge

Regulator: second stage

Depth gauge

Purge valve

The scuba unit

Assembling the equipment

During the early stages of training your instructor will do most of the equipment preparation and assembly. However, as your training progresses you will be expected to take more and more responsibility. Understanding the equipment and developing a logical assembly and check sequence is important for your personal safety.

Attach the BC (buoyancy compensator) to the cylinder, making sure that the BC is positioned correctly, with the cylinder valve outlet facing towards the BC, before tightening the cylinder strap. For best weight carrying, the cylinder should be positioned as high as possible on the back. This will be limited by the need to bend your head backwards without hitting the regulator and cylinder valve. Then stand the cylinder up with the outlet facing away from you and open the cylinder valve momentarily to clear any water or dust from the valve. Before connecting your regulator to the cylinder valve, check that the O-ring seal is in place and undamaged. Connect the first stage by locating the A-clamp or DIN screw into the recess/thread on the cylinder valve. Check that the regulator is positioned correctly and is not

upside-down! Tighten the first stage gently onto the O-ring avoiding excessive force (O-rings require little pressure to seal). Open the cylinder valve slowly, at the same time ensuring that the contents gauge is pointing away from you or anybody else. Ensure the cylinder valve is turned to the fully open position. Check the cylinder pressure by reading the contents gauge (this is sometimes referred to as a submersible pressure gauge or SPG).

Checklist

- Attach BC to cylinder
- Check valve is facing towards BC
- Tighten cylinder strap and check BC is secure
- Stand cylinder up facing away from you
- Clear dust and check O-ring
- Connect first stage
- Check regulator is not upside-down
- Gently tighten first stage connection
- Connect BC hose
- Slowly fully open cylinder valve
- Check contents gauge

Regulator checks

Air supply and contents gauge should be checked

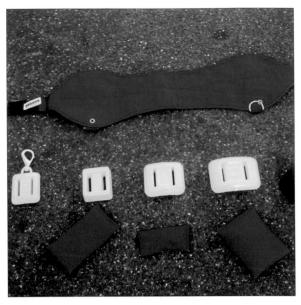

A weight belt and various weights

Regulator checks

It is worth spending time checking your regulator for minor leaks of air. Open the cylinder valve and listen for leaks – an initial, slight leak from the second stage may be stopped by briefly pressing the purge button. Close the cylinder valve and watch the contents gauge. Should the reading fall this is an indication of a leak in the system. Submerging the regulator and cylinder valve assembly and checking for bubble streams can help locate leaks.

Re-open the cylinder valve and take a few breaths from the second stage, at the same time watching the contents gauge. If the needle swings drastically or shows a significant pressure drop this could be an indication of a blocked filter or a cylinder valve not fully open. In either case this must be remedied before the equipment is used. Next, close the cylinder valve and continue to breathe from the regulator. The contents gauge reading should now drop to zero and you should be unable to breathe from the regulator. If you can still inhale there is a leak in the system, possibly in the second stage exhaust valve. Again, this must be remedied before the equipment is used.

Weight checks

Your weight belt may also need some preparation. Depending on the amount of air in their lungs most people have a slight positive buoyancy. This means that, relaxed, you will float at the surface with virtually all your body submerged. Just a small amount of lead weight will allow you to sink. Your weight belt provides this small amount of weight, plus any weight needed to counteract any residual positive buoyancy when all your equipment is taken into account. As the aim is to be neutrally buoyant underwater, it is a mistake to carry either too much or too little weight on your weight belt. Initially, your instructor will advise and help you arrive at the correct loading for your weight belt.

Kitting up

Initial checks complete, you are now ready to put on the equipment. If you have not already done so you should now put on any protective clothing, such as your wetsuit or drysuit. Most divers prefer to leave gloves and hood until just before entering the water. Make sure all your equipment is to hand and not

Buddies assist each other when kitting up

A dive leader talks divers through the dive brief

scattered around in a way that may cause problems for yourself or other divers. Check the BC waist and chest straps are unfastened and loosen off the shoulder straps if they are adjustable.

Fit the weight belt, ensuring that should you need to release it, it will fall free and not snag on any other piece of equipment you will be wearing.

Even when diving in groups, divers use a buddy pairing system as a means of providing immediate assistance should any be needed. This is immediately helpful for the next stage of kitting up. Use your buddy to hold up your scuba unit while you slip into the BC. Avoid trapping regulator hoses and make sure shoulder straps are not twisted. Lean forward and tighten waist fastenings, before pulling down on the shoulder adjusters to tighten them. Next, if fitted, fasten the chest strap with sufficient slack so that the BC can be inflated without causing discomfort.

With the scuba unit in place and secure, check the position of the cylinder by tilting your head back – if your head hits the regulator first stage, the position is too high and the BC cylinder strap will require further adjustment. Now it is your turn to help your buddy.

Once kitting up is complete, the buddy pair should

cross-check each other's equipment, verifying that cylinder valves are fully open and there is sufficient air pressure indicated for the planned dive. Direct feed connections should be checked, as well as BC inflation and deflation and octopus second stage operation. Ensuring each diver understands the operation of his or her buddy's equipment is an important safety factor and this should extend to weight belt and other equipment-release mechanisms.

Dive briefing

Before entering the water it is important that all members of the dive group understand what is planned for the dive. This means that everyone needs to know about entry and exit factors, time and depth limits, the route, planned exercises and equipment operation, communication procedures and any safety concerns. Most of this will have been conveyed during earlier training sessions, but the instructor will give a brief summary highlighting points relevant to the planned dive.

Divers wade out to deeper water at the beginning of a shore dive

Entering the water from a boat

A stride entry from a platform

Entering the water

Immediately before entry, fit the last of your equipment, typically your wetted mask and your fins. It is usually a good idea to have a small amount of air in your BC, enough to ensure some positive buoyancy when you enter the water. You should not enter the water until signalled to do so either by your instructor or the surface-cover controller. Depending on the nature of the dive site, a number of different entry methods can be employed. If you start in shallow water with steps or a ladder for access, you may descend this and fit fins in the water. Similarly, entering from a shelving beach may make it more practical to wade out before fitting fins. Otherwise, it may be easier to wade out to deeper water while wearing your fins by walking backwards. In either case, be careful when negotiating slippery surfaces – until submerged you will be unwieldy as your centre of gravity will have shifted. Make maximum use of the buddy system for mutual support on difficult surfaces and when finally fitting fins.

Probably the most common entry system, particularly from fair-sized dive boats, is the stride entry. This requires sufficiently deep and unobstructed water and is most easily performed from a level platform with a hand support for an upright, fully equipped diver.

Using this method, you stand as close to the platform edge as possible with one hand on the hand-hold. Double-check that the water is clear of obstructions, especially other divers. When the signal is given to go, release the hand-hold and position that hand so as to retain the regulator in your mouth and your mask on your face. At the same time you should take a large stride forward to clear the platform. Try to hit the water in a vertical position. Once the cloud of bubbles from your splash entry subsides, you should find yourself bobbing gently to the surface. Check that your equipment has not become displaced and everything is operating as it should, locate your buddy and confirm everything is okay before turning and signalling 'Okay' to the surface cover. Remember: when you stride forward you have a bulky cylinder strapped to your back, which needs to clear the dive platform as you descend.

Another method of entry is a forward roll – often favoured by photographers as a method of protecting their camera equipment. Starting from a standing

Descending

A backward roll is a common entry method when diving from an inflatable boat

As you descend be sure to equalise your ears before pressure causes discomfort

position, bend your knees and bend forward from the waist, while tucking your chin into your chest and keeping your head as near to your knees as possible. As you roll into the water, the weight of the cylinder will provide momentum so that you enter the water backwards, cylinder-first. One hand remains free for gripping other equipment which is further protected by being held in the chest/stomach area. Until you are used to them, roll methods can be a little disorienting and can sometimes dislodge your mask strap. Make sure you surface clear of the dive platform.

When diving from small boats, which have a low freeboard, a backward roll technique works well. With this type of entry you should sit on the side of the boat and adopt a similar position to the forward roll, check your fins are clear and simply roll backwards into the water. Check your mask strap has not become dislodged before releasing hold of your mask. Otherwise the comments relating to forward roll entries apply. The dive can now begin!

Descending

To descend from the surface you must change from being positively buoyant to neutrally buoyant. It is normal to enter the water with your BC partially inflated so that you are positively buoyant. When ready to descend gradually purge this air until you are neutrally buoyant. If you are correctly weighted – carrying the minimum weight to be neutral at the end of the dive – you should achieve neutral buoyancy just before the BC is totally vented. This is because the weight of the air in your cylinder will make you slightly heavier. When correct weighting and buoyancy are mastered, starting the descent by simply exhaling will usually be possible. When completely submerged you can pivot to continue the descent head first. An alternative is to position yourself horizontally face down at the surface and obtain neutral buoyancy. Then exhale, bend your upper body down underwater and lift your legs straight up in the air. The weight of your legs will drive you downwards. Avoid finning until you are completely submerged, as your fins do not work in air and it will make for a lot of ineffectual splashing and a very untidy start to the dive! Make sure you keep close contact with your buddy and any

Finning in a relaxed and energy-saving style

descent guide rope, such as a shot line or anchor rope while descending, but do not pull yourself down any such guides.

Moving in the water

When finning try to adopt an energy-saving style from the outset. Start by keeping your legs as straight as possible, pivot from the hips and avoid excessive knee bending (bicycling). Some knee bending will always occur, but a fluid finning action involving the whole body and including some hip rotation is much more effective than just knee and ankle movements. Use your hands as little as possible, they are ineffective while fully kitted up and spoil streamlining. Observe how seals swim underwater. You will find that finning when you are completely submerged is more effective than at the surface. If surface swims are necessary, BCs with frontal buoyancy should make swimming on your back more comfortable. However, this has the disadvantage of you not being able to watch where you are going, so frequent over-the-shoulder glances are needed.

Underwater, life is much more comfortable. Here you have true freedom of movement in three dimensions, and happiness is neutral buoyancy. Away from the surface, fins react more effectively with the water. If you are correctly weighted, small changes to the amount of air you breathe in or out can move your overall buoyancy from neutral to negative or positive allowing you to move up or down in the water. Remember, never hold your breath, especially when ascending. With freedom of movement in all dimensions, forward, backward and corkscrew rolls are all possible. You will observe competent divers move through the water with the minimum of effort, making long, slow fin strokes. Body attitude is often controlled by depth of breathing, and hand movements are rare, always kept to a minimum. Keep a safe distance from the sea bed and other underwater objects to avoid con-

Pressure changes

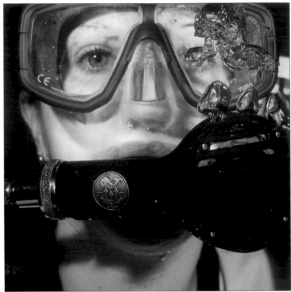

As depth increases so does pressure, divers must equalise the pressure in their ears in order to alleviate pressure differences in air spaces

Developing confidence and familiarity with your regulator is an important diving skill

tact that could damage either yourself or the environment. Be careful when finning that you don't hit your buddy and likewise avoid their fins, as masks and regulators can be dislodged.

Pressure changes

Remember that as you descend you must equalise pressure differences in air spaces. Some divers find it easy to clear ears simply by swallowing, and often only have to clear in the first part of the dive as they descend. Others find it essential to perform nose pinching and blowing whenever descending during a dive. You must not forget to exhale through the nose to balance the pressure in the mask, particularly during the early stages of the descent.

Presuming you were neutrally buoyant at the surface, at a depth of 10m any enclosed volumes of gas will have been reduced by a half due to the increase in pressure. Gas bubbles in a foam neoprene suit will be affected and the suit's buoyancy considerably reduced. A corresponding volume of air from the direct feed will have to be allowed into your BC in order to regain neutral buoyancy. Divers wearing drysuits will expe-

rience a similar reduction in buoyancy as the air in the suit is compressed. Besides loss of buoyancy, this can create an uncomfortable or even painful squeeze. The remedy is simple, bleed air from the direct feed into the suit at intervals during your descent, always seeking to keep your buoyancy close to neutral.

Breathing

To best enjoy your diving in complete safety, you need to develop familiarity with, and confidence in, the equipment and techniques you will be using. A key piece of equipment is your regulator. Initially this will probably be fitted and checked for you, but as your diving progresses you will do this yourself. Using the regulator is relatively straightforward, it is just a matter of holding the mouthpiece bite pegs between your teeth and sealing your lips around the outside of the mouthpiece. Once in the water it should feel comfortable and be easy to breathe from, whatever your attitude or depth, as long as the feed hose is positioned correctly. If at the end of the dive your jaw is aching, it will probably be because you are gripping it too hard. Don't worry, this is not uncommon at the

A diver practises using his buddy's alternate air source

beginning of your diver training, on your next dive just try to relax the pressure you are exerting.

At an early stage in your training you will be taught how to remove the mouthpiece from your mouth while underwater and then replace it without surfacing. This is not difficult – either use the regulator purge button to clear the small amount of water which will enter the mouthpiece, or simply blow it out yourself.

As a skill, regulator removal and replacement is important, because it teaches you the basis of how to replace your primary regulator with either your own or your buddy's alternate air source (AAS) should the need ever arise. You will be taught regulator recovery techniques such as sweeping an arm behind you or adopting a head-down position should the regulator swing completely out of your field of view.

It is a small step from removing and replacing your own regulator underwater, to learning how to breathe from your buddy's AAS. When using this technique positioning and contact are the keys to success. You need to be positioned so that the AAS regulator is correctly, comfortably and securely fitted in your mouth, and ideally so that you and your buddy have eye contact with each other. As you are now using a breathing source fitted to your buddy, there must be secure contact between the pair of you. Such an event will mean the termination of the dive, and you both must be able to ascend safely and comfortably.

Mask clearing

Hold the top of the mask against your face and tilt your head backwards

As you gently exhale, the water in the mask will be forced out of the bottom of the mask skirt

Mask clearing

Another early skill to master is that of emptying water out of your dive mask without surfacing, a technique called mask clearing. While masks are normally quite watertight, there are occasions when water can seep in. Altering your facial shape by smiling or laughing – both of which are possible underwater – can cause leaks. So, too, can a poor seal under the nose for those with a moustache. Consequently, another important and confidence-building skill you will be taught is that of mask clearing. The principle is very simple. Position yourself to be head-up so that the dive mask faceplate is vertical, then tilt your head slightly backwards. Any water inside the mask will obey the pull of gravity and collect at the bottom of the mask in and around the nose pocket, not a problem because you are inhaling with your mouth. In this position exhale gently from your nose, so the air will bubble up through the water in your mask, pressurising it to force the water out of the bottom of the mask skirt, where the seal is weakest. Correctly performed, as soon as you see bubbles escaping up past the outside of your mask, all the water that was inside the mask will have been expelled. There are various preferred methods of holding masks while clearing, some of which are shown in the diagrams (left).

This same procedure works equally well with a small amount of water or a mask full of water. In fact, you will learn to cope with both situations and progress to completely removing, replacing and then clearing your mask underwater. Sometimes people have a little difficulty in maintaining a normal breathing rhythm when first learning this skill. To automatically hold your breath when your nose becomes submerged is a natural human protective response. You have to learn to override this reflex and continue to breathe from the regulator in your mouth while sealing off the nasal passages. The easiest way to do this is to stand or kneel in shallow water, breathing through your mouth from your regulator but without a dive mask, and then to put your face in the water while continuing to breathe normally. After a few tries you will master the technique of continuing to breathe with your nose exposed to the water and are ready to complete the technique of mask clearing.

Mask clearing allows you to remove
any water that may have entered
your mask

Buoyancy

A neutrally buoyant diver

Learning buoyancy skills

Buoyancy

One of the joys of diving is the weightlessness of neutral buoyancy. To fully enjoy this aspect of diving the learner diver should master buoyancy control as early as possible. Good buoyancy control at all stages of a dive is essential for safety reasons. With a small amount of instruction, this is not a difficult task and once mastered will pay you back for the rest of your diving career. You must develop a concept of yourself and your equipment as a small submarine. To remain at the surface the gravitational force pulling you down must be exceeded by the upward force of the water that is trying not to be displaced by your presence. The upward force of the water depends directly on the volume displaced – the submerged portion of yourself and your equipment – so any changes in that volume that do not involve a change in your weight will change your state of buoyancy. If you increase your overall volume the upthrust will increase and you will be more buoyant. If you decrease your overall volume the upthrust will decrease and you will tend to sink

There are two principal means of changing your volume, using your body or using your diving equipment. Every time you breathe in and out you

effectively change your volume, the actual amount of volume change depending upon the extent of your inhalation or exhalation. This is termed your tidal volume and in a relaxed state will be of the order of about 0.5 litres. Assuming your torso is submerged this will create a change in your displacement of 0.5 litres and thus a change of upthrust of 0.5kg (1 litre of water weighs 1kg). Because of the density of water, you experience a fair amount of resistance in moving through it, so in practice there is a degree of time lag before small changes of buoyancy produce any significant upwards or downwards movement. So, with a normal breathing depth and rate, this means inertia will dampen out any tendency to yo-yo up and down in the water. On the other hand, larger inhalations and exhalations will have a proportionally greater effect and can initiate vertical movement.

Another factor used to affect buoyancy is to change the amount of air retained in your lungs over and above the tidal air. If you inhale deeply and then control your breathing at a relatively small tidal level (using shallow breaths), your overall volume will have increased and you will tend to float upwards.

This technique is sometimes referred to as 'breathing off the top' of your lungs. It is used to help temporarily lift yourself should you inadvertently become too close to the sea bed, your buddy or some other object. It is a technique to be used carefully and should not in any way be allowed to lead to a dangerous breath-holding ascent. It is also a major part of the reason you tend to need more weight at the start of your diving career. In the early stages of your diving there is a natural tendency to want to hold your breath underwater, and to initially inhale a larger amount of air than normal. At this stage you are not accustomed to having a breathing source underwater, and will also tend to take shorter and more rapid breaths. The opposite of this technique is to reduce your buoyancy by exhaling more deeply than normal and then to 'breathe off the bottom' of your lungs. This can be used to help initiate a descent or temporarily avoid an overhead obstruction such as your buddy or an obstacle. Being able to change buoyancy, and therefore position in the water, in this manner is particularly advantageous when the use of your fins is restricted, such as when you are too close to a silty sea bed, a buddy or other obstruction.

The second method of buoyancy control is by altering your overall volume by means of an external piece of diving equipment. Normally this would be your BC or, if worn, drysuit. It is easy to see that introducing air into either of these enclosed spaces will increase their volume, thus increasing the amount of water they displace. In turn, this will increase the upward-acting force on them and result in an increase in your overall buoyancy. Similarly by venting air from your BC or drysuit you will decrease their volume, creating less upthrust and so have less buoyancy. To avoid unwanted rapid upward or downward movements take care to control the amounts of air you allow in or out of such equipment.

It is worth noting that changing depth will also change the volume of air in your BC or drysuit, as the ambient water pressure increases or decreases. If you add air to become more buoyant, you may rise through the water thus decreasing the ambient pressure, which will allow the air to expand creating still more upthrust. This will cause your upward movement to accelerate and if care is not taken to vent excess air an uncontrolled ascent can result.

Venting air will tend to produce the same effect, but in the opposite direction. As you descend, air in your BC or drysuit compresses, thereby reducing buoyancy and accelerating the descent. Unless air is added to correct the negative buoyancy an uncontrolled descent can occur, causing either your planned depth limits to be exceeded or for you to collide with the bottom – or both!

This may sound a little daunting, but if you understand the principles a little practise in the water will soon see you in complete control of your buoyancy. A good exercise for all divers is to fine tune your buoyancy so you can hover motionless in mid-water, able to sense the slight upward and downward movement as you breathe gently in and out. Many divers perform this by 'sitting' cross-legged holding their fin tips in an underwater yoga like position.

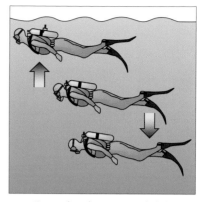

Increasing the amount of air in your lungs or BC increases your buoyancy, when you decrease the amount of air in your lungs or BC your buoyancy decreases

Ascending

Making a safety stop before ascending to the surface

A diver hands over his equipment before entering the boat

Ascending

The key word during an ascent is control. Breath-holding can be potentially dangerous, so make sure your breathing is normal. Maintain neutral buoyancy by controlled venting of your BC or drysuit if necessary. If you are too heavy, upward progress is difficult and hard finning will be required. If you are too light, the speed of ascent will be difficult to control. Remember that the closer you get to the surface the more rapid the change in pressure so the more rapid the expansion of any air in buoyancy devices, drysuits and lungs. A safety stop at 6m to check buoyancy control is good practice. When you get close to the surface listen and look to avoid surface craft and obstructions. In poor visibility a hand raised high can help protect you from striking your head on unseen obstructions. Ascending face-to-face with your buddy enables good visual contact with each other for communications and you can each scan opposite areas for potential hazards, especially when breaking the surface. On arrival at the surface, continue to keep a look out before checking 'Okay' with your buddy and the surface cover party.

Leaving the water

All good things must come to an end and at some stage the dive will have to end. As part of any dive plan the exit procedure should be understood by the divers. Remember, swimming on the surface is more difficult than underwater. With good navigation most of the return should be possible underwater. The whole idea is to go diving, not swimming! Once the surface has been reached, ensure positive buoyancy by inflating your BC. The exit point will frequently be the same as or close to the entry point. If this is shore-based it will normally be the reverse of the entry procedure. It is important to work as a team with your buddy to clear the water and remove equipment.

If returning to a boat, make sure the boat knows you are there and all propeller movement is stopped. Then approach the boarding point or the point where equipment will be handed in prior to boarding.

Some dive boats have a specially designed ladder, with rungs projecting each side of a central spine. These ladders often extend underwater and are angled to make it easy to climb. This type can be ascended fully kitted, making diver recovery quick and simple and the divers can remove equipment in the boat,

Divers should retain their regulators in their mouths until back on board the boat

Using a ladder to climb back on board the boat

again this is best performed with buddy assistance.

Conventional ladders are more difficult for equipped divers to climb and it is usual to hold on to the ladder, remove fins and hand them a member of the surface cover on the boat before climbing the ladder. If the ladder climb is difficult, it may be advisable to remove and hand in your weight belt and possibly even remove your scuba unit, letting the surface cover haul this in while you climb the ladder.

To gain entry into small boats such as rigid inflatable boats (RIBs) it is usual to keep your fins on, but remove and hand in your weight belt and scuba unit. You can then submerge a little, retaining a firm hold of the boat, before finning up strongly and at the same time pulling yourself up and into the boat.

In all exits remember that once you have removed the scuba unit you lose an air source and your prime source of buoyancy. Also, once you remove your fins you will find your mobility in the water is drastically reduced. Always try to keep your regulator in your mouth as long as possible, even until you are back in the boat and retain your mask in place while in the water. Save the talking until back on board!

After the dive

Back on dry land you can relive your dive, discuss it with your dive buddy and see what you can take from the experience to help you enjoy future dives even more. Before this happens, record your air cylinder's end-of-dive pressure and dismantle and stow away your equipment safely, in a manner that will not cause problems for other divers. If it is possible to rinse your equipment in fresh water, this should be done at the earliest opportunity. Check back to see how accurately you were able to adhere to your dive plan, particularly regarding planned depth and time. Finally, make a record of the dive in your dive logbook. This logged experience record will be a pleasure to you in the future and will also allow other dive centres to see the extent of your experience. □

Chapter three

Breaking the surface

Having learned the basic skills and made the first of your early dives, it's time to take a look around. The visibility underwater will have a big effect on your diving. While some divers prefer to dive in clear water, others enjoy the challenge of successfully completing a dive in low visibility. Light and the weather also play their part in unwrapping stunning sights for those prepared to enter the underwater world.

Breaking the surface
Visibility

Organisms and sedimentary matter can cause poor visibility

In good visibility magnificent seascapes are revealed

Where land-bound people talk of the weather, divers talk about the visibility. You might think that water temperature is the prime concern, but in fact it is the distance you can see that is a major distinction between dive sites and individual dives. As the whole point is to observe a different world, this is hardly surprising. So what are the factors influencing our ability to see underwater? Given reasonable eyesight (possibly corrected by lenses) and a good mask, there remain the amount of light and the water itself as variables. The amount of light is obviously important. The changing elevation of the sun at different times of the day means light penetration also differs, with midday giving the strongest lighting for most sites. Cloud cover will also affect underwater lighting.

Water absorbs the light, so the deeper you go, the less light there is available. Lack of light can be compensated for by lights carried by the diver. Many

divers carry a waterproof torch to light up darker crevices or even to enable diving at night.

The biggest influence on underwater visibility is the material suspended in the water. Sedimentary matter and minute living organisms in the water can block our vision, rather like a fog. The sedimentary matter in the sea frequently comes from material flushed into the vicinity from local rivers. The areas affected vary, depending on both the size and hinterland of the river, and according to inland rains.

Tidal conditions can also change the flow of a river, giving differing visibility at different states of the tide. Storms can also raise sediment from the sea bed, especially in shallow waters, and adversely affect visibility until the silt settles.

The way in which visibility is affected by marine organisms tends to be more a function of climate and geography. There is a food chain underwater with a

Good visibility can make a major contribution
to the enjoyment of a dive

Food chain

Some mammals, such as dolphins, feed on fish

The shy basking shark feeds on plankton

base of plant life using sunlight to gain its life energy through photosynthesis. To exploit the vast areas of the oceans, plant life has evolved in both fixed and free-floating forms. These floating forms affect our underwater visibility. The often microscopic plants are in turn used as a food source by minute animals, frequently the young or larval forms of other sea creatures, and these in turn will also reduce visibility. As the plant life is using light as its basic energy source there are optimum conditions where this can be successful. Too little light means the plankton cannot survive, and too much can also have an adverse effect. The water temperature also has a role to play in providing the most suitable growth conditions.

This means that there tends to be a depth zone where plankton growth will be prolific, and hence visibility reduced. This zone often varies in depth depending on the time of day or strength of the sunlight, and is found deeper at midday than early morning or late afternoon. At night, the plankton layer is often found at the surface and can provide spectacular electroluminescent effects as divers' movements leave phosphorescent trails in the water.

As plankton is climate-sensitive, divers will often come into contact with plankton 'blooms', when waters are filled with newborn plankton. This is especially so in temperate waters, where spring and autumn blooms create periods when the underwater visibility is drastically reduced.

The drifting plankton provides a food source for a wide range of other marine creatures, ranging from the smallest of fish right through to enormous whales. In turn, many of the plankton-eating fish are the main food source for other fish, even to the extent that adult forms prey on junior forms of the same species. So, while divers often grumble about poor visibility, this cloudy murk is a basic food source for the fish life we want to see during our underwater excursions.

A feeding tubeworm

Lobsters tend to hide in rocky crevices

Plant and animal life

Not all marine life is free swimming. Many underwater life forms spend their existence attached to rocky walls or to the sea bed. Some of these life forms are plants, such as the beautiful forests of kelp found in temperate waters, or the savannahs of sea grass in seas such as the Mediterranean. Others, while superficially appearing to be plants, are actually animals, such as the community dwelling corals of the tropics or the many coloured sponges and siphons. These sedentary colonies often form the basis of an undersea habitat for other life forms, providing either a food source or shelter or both. Many varieties of shellfish are also bottom dwelling, some preferring to grow attached to rocky surfaces, others preferring to be hidden in the sand or mud. Crustacea such as crabs, crayfish and lobsters hide in rocky crevices, while starfish, sea cucumbers and the more mobile shellfish roam the bottom, grazing on kelp, sea grass or coral. Marine biology is a massive and fascinating science and many divers, having seen the wonderful forms of life underwater, become totally captivated by its study.

It is worth mentioning here that while in the beginning diving itself may be totally absorbing, it is really not an end in itself. Learning to dive is learning a new form of movement, just like walking, riding a bicycle or flying an aeroplane. Once you have learned to dive you have the ability to enter this strange and wonderful region of our planet. And as with walking, you can use this ability for many associated activities and at many levels. You can enjoy the undersea equivalents of walking on moors, climbing mountains, exploring jungles. You can enjoy the scenery and photograph, film or video it to reinforce memories. You can simply admire or study in depth the plants and creatures you encounter. Because of the more limited visibility we experience, underwater panoramas are necessarily more restricted than above the surface. However, they can be just as spectacular, with underwater cliffs, arches, caverns and boulder fields to delight the eye and intrigue those with an interest in geology.

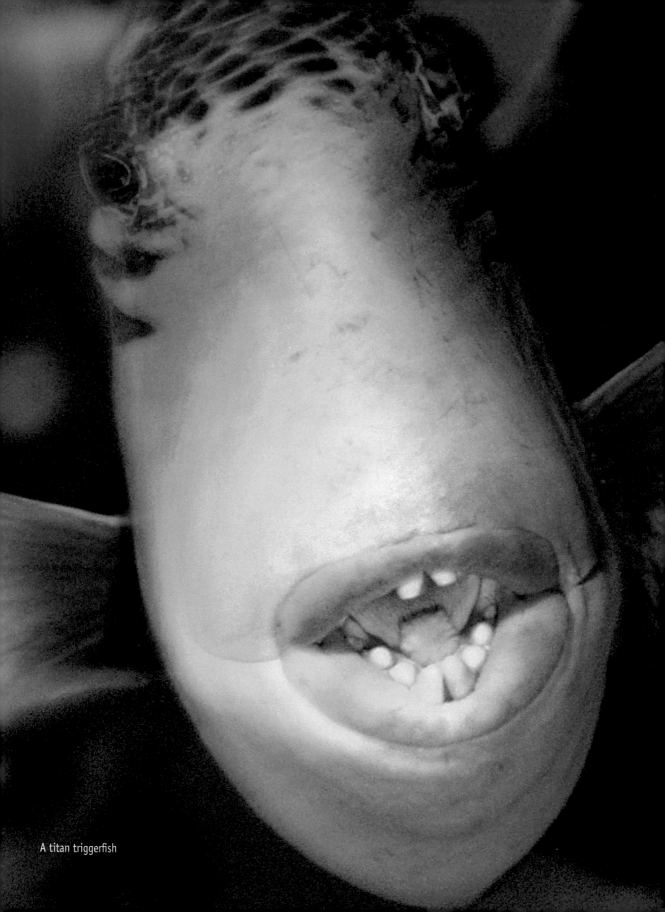

A titan triggerfish

Look, don't touch!

Diving is your new form of transport, providing you with privileged access to the underwater world, and it is important that you do not abuse that privilege, even inadvertently, by lack of knowledge or skill. Equally, you do not want to expose yourself or others to unnecessary risk. By entering this world you can create a potentially damaging imbalance unless you understand the effects of your intrusion. The ideal is to take only memories, and as a diver underwater you have the opportunity to do that without even leaving footprints! Be careful that careless finning does not cause physical damage to what are often delicate plants or animals. Avoid damaging things by unnecessary contact. Plants and animals underwater are constantly striving to be successful and survive, and certain organisms develop quite powerful defence mechanisms and strategies to help in life's battle. Some of these defences can have unpleasant or even dangerous effects on humans, such as stings from fire coral or jellyfish, the poisonous spines of stonefish or lionfish, or attacks by territorial triggerfish.

While unprovoked attacks from larger fish are extremely rare, even minor cuts and wounds from sharp or spiny objects underwater can take a long time to heal and should be carefully cleaned to avoid infection. The simple rule that benefits both the marine environment and the diver is: 'Look, but don't touch'.

While on the subject of avoiding possible problems, it is worth remembering that at some stage in the dive it will be necessary to return to the surface. With this in mind you should always be conscious of situations which could obstruct a direct ascent by creating a 'no-clear surface' situation. This obviously happens if you are tempted to enter a shipwreck or cavern, but even boulders and rock arches and overhangs can obstruct your route to the surface. Exploring such obstructed areas requires the use of additional safety techniques and more advanced training. Therefore, be careful to avoid places requiring such special penetration diving techniques until you have gained the right training and experience.

You should also try to develop an awareness of the changes to your profile once you are dressed in all your equipment. Your girth is enlarged by the addition of your dive cylinder, and your length is increased by wearing fins, while gauges and hoses also protrude to increase the space you occupy. This enlarged space is

Moray eels are generally not dangerous, but may bite any hands that stray into the crevices or holes in which they live

what you have to consider when swimming close to other divers, cliffs, the sea bed or other underwater objects. Stirring up the sea bed with careless fin strokes is not environmentally friendly and can ruin the visibility, even to the extent of making enclosed areas dangerous. It is embarrassing to be brought to an abrupt halt because a trailing contents gauge or some other dangling piece of equipment has become entangled in the coral, shipwreck or rocks you were swimming over. With the restricted angle of vision imposed by your dive mask, this embarrassment can be downright dangerous if you cannot see to free yourself, so keep hoses and other dangly bits tucked away and secured as close to your body as possible. □

Chapter four

Deeper in knowledge

While some of the effects of pressure, such as the need to equalise, are easily recognisable, others require a more in-depth understanding of human physiology. When we are underwater, nitrogen bubbles in the bloodstream can have a significant impact on our bodies and, if correct procedures are not followed, can lead to instances of decompression illness. However, an understanding of how our bodies work will lead to safer and more enjoyable diving.

Deeper in knowledge
Breathing freely

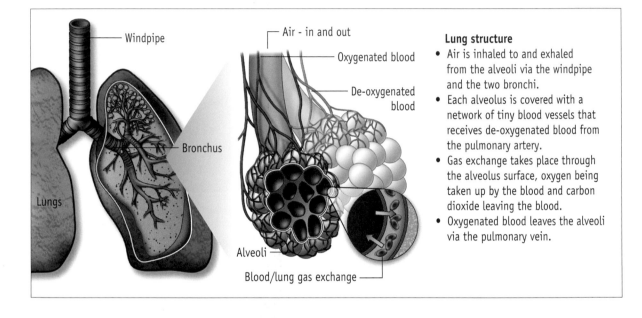

Windpipe

Bronchus

Lungs

Air - in and out

Oxygenated blood

De-oxygenated blood

Alveoli

Blood/lung gas exchange

Lung structure
- Air is inhaled to and exhaled from the alveoli via the windpipe and the two bronchi.
- Each alveolus is covered with a network of tiny blood vessels that receives de-oxygenated blood from the pulmonary artery.
- Gas exchange takes place through the alveolus surface, oxygen being taken up by the blood and carbon dioxide leaving the blood.
- Oxygenated blood leaves the alveoli via the pulmonary vein.

Our bodies consist of a variety of cells, all of which perform particular functions that enable us to exist. In turn, these individual cells require energy to live and operate. They obtain this energy through a process called 'metabolism', where oxygen is used to 'burn' food, thus creating energy and some by-products.

**Food + oxygen =
energy + water + carbon dioxide + waste products**

It is the job of the bloodstream to deliver food and oxygen to the cells and then to remove by-products. The heart acts as a pump to circulate the blood between the vital organs and the rest of our body cells, where the necessary gas and chemical interchanges can be made. Food is made available by regular eating and subsequent digestion and storage, while oxygen intake and carbon dioxide expulsion are achieved by the breathing cycle. Excess water and other cellular waste products are removed via the excretory system.

As divers, it is our breathing mechanism that is most affected by our underwater activity and therefore this requires a fuller understanding. Respiration is the process of inhaling air (or another breathing gas that contains sufficient oxygen) into the lungs via the mouth or nose and then exhaling the unused parts of this gas along with the carbon dioxide produced by the cells. The surface of the lungs brings our bloodstream, flowing through tiny capillaries, into close contact with the inhaled gases in the alveoli.

In the alveoli, some of the oxygen from the inhaled air diffuses into the blood and, similarly, carbon

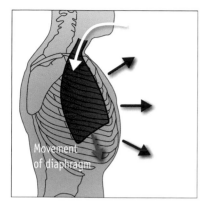

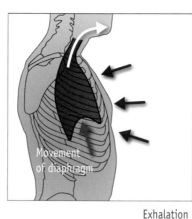

Inhalation

Exhalation

Inhalation (far left) As you breathe in, your ribs are pushed outwards and your diaphragm is tightened, thus pulling it downwards. These actions expand the chest cavity, causing the lungs to draw air in through the mouth or nose.
Exhalation (left) Breathing out is the reverse of this process, the ribs moving inwards and the diaphragm upwards, shrinking the chest cavity and expelling air from the lungs.

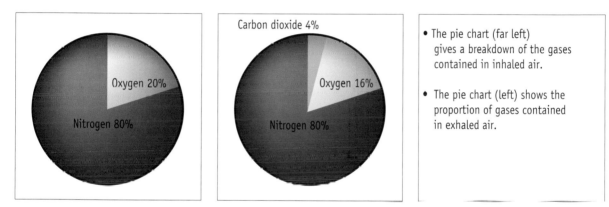

Inhaled air

Exhaled air

- The pie chart (far left) gives a breakdown of the gases contained in inhaled air.

- The pie chart (left) shows the proportion of gases contained in exhaled air.

dioxide diffuses out of the blood into the alveoli.

The air we breathe is made up of a number of gases in various proportions. Nitrogen, a normally inert gas, forms the largest part at roughly 80 per cent. When we breathe this in and out, it usually has no effect on our living processes. Oxygen is the next largest constituent, at around 20 per cent. The amount and pressure of oxygen in the air we normally inhale is more than we need and only about four per cent of it is involved in our living processes, the rest is simply breathed out along with the nitrogen and carbon dioxide. The percentages of nitrogen and oxygen listed here are approximate and there are also traces of other gases in the atmosphere, but these are very tiny and usually play no active role in our respiration.

On land, changes in either the mixture of gases that we breathe, or the way in which we breathe, can cause us problems. The same applies while diving, but we must always bear in mind that because we are underwater, the consequences can be much more serious. Contaminants such as carbon monoxide from exhaust fumes can have serious physiological effects when breathed at the surface. Even small quantities can have enhanced effects if breathed at depth under pressure.

Air consumption

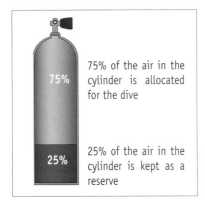

75% of the air in the cylinder is allocated for the dive

25% of the air in the cylinder is kept as a reserve

How long will it last?

Living in an environment of air, we don't pay much attention to its availability, but that certainly has to change when it comes to diving. The amount of air we carry in our cylinders is one of the crucial limitations on our diving. As mentioned earlier, air is compressed at very high pressure in order that we can carry as much as possible in a cylinder of manageable size. A cylinder with an internal volume of 10 litres, filled with air compressed at 200 bar, will contain (10 litres x 200 =) 2,000 litres of air at normal atmospheric pressure. To establish how much air we use during a dive we need to understand something about our bodies' respiration and oxygen usage. A typical adult will have a total lung volume of around 6 litres. However, as we cannot totally empty our lungs and rarely fully inflate them, this is an academic amount. What we need to know is how much air we actually breathe in (and out), and can therefore be said to have consumed over a set period of time. Your air consumption will vary, depending on your activity at the time. Sitting reading this book, you are probably breathing in and out about 0.5 litres with each breath and taking about 12 breaths each minute. That gives an air-consumption figure of (0.5 litres x 12 =) 6 litres a minute and would allow you to breathe from the 10-litre cylinder pressurised to 200 bar for (2,000 litres ÷ 6 litres =) 333 minutes. Engaging in more strenuous activity, such as swimming, will increase both your depth and rate of breathing, and consequently increase your air-consumption rate. The exact rate is going to vary with the intensity of the physical effort and will also vary from person to person, with factors such as size and fitness being significant. When diving, we take a consumption rate of 25 litres per minute as a planning guide. While it is possible to exceed this rate, it is also possible to conduct dives at below this figure, so it is important to analyse your diving habits to see if this is a reasonable figure for your own dive planning. Typically, air consumption is high in the early stages of learning to dive and then reduces to a steady level with more experience and improved technique. Experienced divers may well find rates such as 15 litres per minute more usual.

Ambient pressure

We must also take into account how the depth of a dive affects the ambient pressure. As our depth increases so does the surrounding pressure, and consequently the regulator delivers air to us at higher pressure. At 10m the ambient pressure is doubled, so we need to breathe air at 2 bar to balance that external water pressure. This means each breath we take consumes twice as much air as that same breath at the surface – effectively doubling our air-consumption rate. At a depth of 20m we have an ambient pressure of 3 bar, and the air we breathe needs to be at 3 bar. Three times as much air occupies the same lung volume as at the surface and our air-consumption rate becomes (25 litres x 3 =) 75 litres per minute. Obviously we must then take into account depth as well as breathing rate when we plan how long a particular air supply might last. Our 2,000-litre supply will only last (2,000 litres ÷ 25 litres ÷ 3 =) 26.7 minutes when diving at 20m (3 bar) and breathing at 25 litres per minute. This is a fairly crude calculation as not all of the dive would be spent at that depth and you would obviously not want to end the dive at 20m with no air.

You should plan to arrive back at the surface with some reserve of air in the cylinder. There are many factors to take into account in deciding what is a sensible reserve for a particular dive. Reasonable rules of thumb at this stage are to consider either 50-bar pressure or 25 per cent of the air supply as suitable amounts.

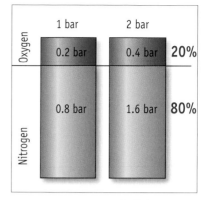

Partial pressures

Partial pressures

To best understand the effects that the gases we breathe have on us, we need to appreciate the effects of pressure on the gases themselves. At the earth's surface the atmospheric pressure is about 1 bar, and each of the gases forming the atmosphere contributes proportionately to creating that pressure. Therefore, the nitrogen contributes some 80 per cent or 0.8 bar and the oxygen about 20 per cent or 0.2 bar. These are called the 'partial pressures' of the various gases. Within a fully charged air cylinder, with the air compressed to 200 bar, the partial pressure of the nitrogen will be approximately (200 x 0.8 =) 160 bar and the oxygen partial pressure (200 x 0.2 =) 40 bar. As the regulator supplies us with breathing gas at the pressure of the water surrounding us, it follows that the partial pressures of the gases we inhale will vary, depending on the depth we are at. So at 10m the ambient pressure is 2 bar and we will inhale breathing gas at 2 bar. If this is normal compressed air, the nitrogen will form (2 x 0.8 =) 1.6 bar and the oxygen (2 x 0.2 =) 0.4 bar – or double the partial pressure we are used to at the surface. Our bodies are quite used to breathing in an excess of oxygen, and the excess is simply breathed out – the cells of our body simply take what they need.

Oxygen

Divers should check their air consumption by reading their contents gauges frequently

Too much of a good thing

Although the amount of oxygen your body takes in increases at depth, this is of no importance as long as the increase is relatively small, but it is possible to have too much of a good thing. At the surface, 100-percent oxygen is often used to treat a variety of medical problems. As a result of such use, it has been found that there are limits to our tolerance of excess oxygen, both in time exposure and quantity. Prolonged exposure to oxygen can produce convulsions and unconsciousness, so its use underwater is restricted to special circumstances. Similarly, the use of special breathing-gas mixtures such as nitrox, sometimes called enriched air, where the oxygen content is artificially increased, requires special precautions and training in their use and limitations. A particular limitation is depth, because as depth – and therefore pressure – increases, so does the partial pressure of the oxygen content, eventually to potentially dangerous levels. Many diver training agencies advise a maximum oxygen partial pressure of 1.4 bar for underwater use. If the oxygen level in the breathing gas mixture increased to 40 per cent (double the normal level) then the 1.4 bar limit would be reached with an ambient pressure of 3.5 bar, a depth of 25m. It is interesting to note that this same limit applied to normal air is reached at 7 bar ambient or 60m.

Too little is also bad

While the air that we breathe – either compressed or at atmospheric pressure – provides us with a more than ample quantity of oxygen, we need to understand the consequences of oxygen deprivation. Getting oxygen from our breathing supply to our cells involves a long and complex chain and it is worth considering each of the links in turn. Our normal breathing-gas supply is the atmosphere, and as long as it is not contaminated with pollutants causes no real supply problem. While diving we depend on the limited gas supply from our cylinder and the correct functioning of our regulator. A contents gauge indicates the quantity of gas in the cylinder and regulators are designed and built to be highly reliable, robust devices with mainly fail-safe operation, as long as they are treated properly and serviced according to the manufacturers' guidelines.

It is good practice to keep your regulator in your mouth, even at the surface

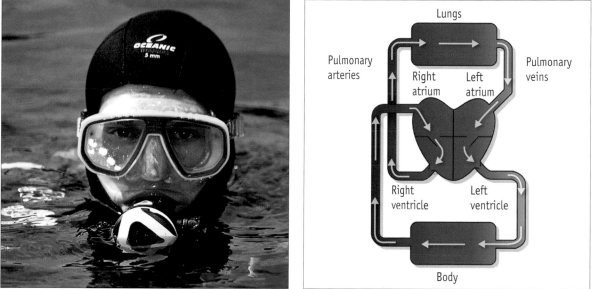

The human circulatory system

Air supply failures as a result of faulty equipment are very rare. Failure caused by divers' poor monitoring of their contents gauges is regrettably less rare. We also need to be sure that the gas we are breathing contains an appropriate amount of oxygen. As long as the gas is compressed air there should be no problem, but if the gas is artificially mixed (such as nitrox) then the oxygen content must be verified at all stages of production and immediately prior to use. Having established what gas we are breathing, the next stage of oxygen intake comes through our breathing passages – the air-filled spaces of our lungs, mouth and nose. As the nose is usually enclosed in the diving face mask, inhalation and most exhalation is via the mouth. Provided the regulator is in the mouth, and there are no obstructions in the mouth, throat or lungs, there should be no problems with oxygen supply. It is worth developing the habit of keeping your regulator in place in your mouth all the while you are in the water and resist the temptation to chat with your buddy unnecessarily while at the surface – wait until you are out of the water.

Once in the lungs the oxygen is transferred from the alveoli to the bloodstream where, combined with the haemoglobin of the red cells, it is carried around the rest of the body. The efficiency of these links in the chain depends on the health of the lungs, the heart and the blood and circulatory system. Any respiratory disease affecting the lungs can also affect the proper transfer of oxygen into the bloodstream. It is wise to get a knowledgeable medical opinion on any serious or persistent respiratory conditions and to avoid diving when suffering from minor respiratory ailments. Of course, smoking is known to damage the lungs and should be avoided by divers, especially just before or after a dive. The heart is the pump which moves the blood around the body and plays a vital role in keeping our body cells adequately supplied with oxygen. Any disease which reduces the efficiency of the heart can have a direct and adverse effect on that oxygen supply. Once again a non-smoking policy is advisable.

The liquid part of the blood known as plasma, carries in solution the complex sugars used as food by the

Hypoxia and anoxia

Using decompression tables correctly will minimise the risk of decompression illness

cells, as well as other salts and proteins needed by the body. Within the liquid are suspended the oxygen-carrying red blood cells, mixed with the disease-fighting white blood cells and the platelets used in clotting to prevent bleeding. The red blood cells are actually tinged blue by the haemoglobin, until it combines with oxygen to form the red oxy-haemoglobin. This makes the arterial blood pumped from the heart to the tissues its healthy red colour, while the venous blood returning to the heart and lungs with its reduced oxygen content is much bluer in colour. Diseases affecting the blood, particularly anaemia with its associated reduced-red cell count, can also reduce the supply of oxygen to the cells.

Hypoxia and anoxia

A reduction in the oxygen supply to the cells can produce hypoxic symptoms. Firstly, as all the available oxygen is removed by the cells from the blood, it will become progressively bluer. This will cause the skin to lose its normal pinkness and will be particularly visible in the lips and nail beds. A shortage of oxygen is called 'hypoxia' and will cause impaired functioning of the cells, producing fatigue and mental confusion as

the brain cells are affected, followed by unconsciousness and convulsions. If the situation is not rectified rapidly, permanent cell damage can occur. The brain cells are especially sensitive and if deprived of oxygen for as little as four minutes can be irreversibly damaged. A condition referred to as 'anoxia', occurs when there is no available oxygen and unless immediately corrected will lead to death.

Nitrogen and diving

When we breathe nitrogen at the surface it is considered to be inert. However, when we dive, nitrogen has considerable effects on our bodies. Breathing 80-percent nitrogen, the gas dissolves in our body tissues normally until a saturated state is reached, which has no apparent effect on us. However, when we dive, the nitrogen in the compressed air we breathe is at a higher partial pressure and this causes our body tissues to absorb still more of the gas. If we remained at a particular depth for long enough our tissues would again become saturated at that pressure, but the important factors are that the higher the ambient pressure and the longer the dive duration, the more nitrogen is absorbed. Absorption occurs for most of the dive and it is not until we reduce the ambient pressure and reach the final stages of the ascent that this process starts to reverse. In a properly conducted dive this absorption and release of nitrogen by our body tissues occurs without us being aware of the process. However, it is important to realise that most of the dive is spent absorbing nitrogen and that the final off-gassing ascent phase is relatively short. Divers usually arrive back at the surface with considerably higher than normal nitrogen loadings in their tissues. Over a period of time this will reduce back to a normal level. This process is referred to as 'decompressing' and we must understand that all dives in which we are exposed to increased ambient pressure involve a compression phase followed by a decompression phase.

Nitrogen and decompression illness

As long as the ascent phase is not too rapid for the quantity of nitrogen we have absorbed, decompression occurs without adverse effect. If the rate of change of pressure is too great, decompression illness (DCI) can result. Here, instead of being carried in solution back to the lungs where it can be expired, nitrogen

Precautionary safety stops at the end of a dive will help to dissipate nitrogen bubbles

bubbles form in the body tissues. These bubbles can damage the tissues they are in, as well as obstructing blood supplies and damaging surrounding tissues. Once formed, the bubbles can grow as further nitrogen is released, and such situations call for immediate medical treatment if permanent damage is to be avoided. Treatment will normally involve the administration of 100-per-cent oxygen and transportation to recompression facilities where the casualty can be recompressed to reduce the size of the offending bubbles and receive appropriate medical treatment. The earlier the treatment, the greater the chance of its success, so any symptoms should be evaluated seriously and reacted to appropriately.

Fortunately there are relatively simple strategies that can be adopted to minimise the risk of DCI being a problem. As the main factors causing the nitrogen to be absorbed are depth and time, a close watch can be kept on these parameters to ensure safe limits are not exceeded. These limits are laid down in decompression tables that can be used as part of the dive planning process (see appendix one). As a further safeguard, divers frequently carry a dive computer which constantly monitors the diver's exposure to pressure and the duration of that exposure. Clever programming allows the device to inform the wearer of their decompression status and appropriate ascent procedures. Early dives in your training will be relatively shallow and will not last long, so the risk of decompression problems is small, but it is a good

Nitrogen

Hyperbaric chambers are used in the treatment of decompression sickness

Decompression illness – symptoms

- Itches and rashes
- Joint aches and pains
- Numbness and tingling sensation
- Dizziness, visual disturbance
- Confusion, nausea, headaches
- Shortness of breath
- Chest pain or discomfort
- Crepitation (generally, bubbles under the skin around the upper chest or neck)
- Voice change
- General fatigue, weakness or paralysis
- Unconsciousness

Many of these symptoms can be associated with either too rapid release of nitrogen from the body tissue, or burst lung problems. Correct diagnosis is unimportant at the first-aid stage as treatment is identical. The casualty requires urgent evacuation to a recompression facility and skilled medical attention. During and while awaiting evacuation the breathing of 100% oxygen is beneficial, though may result in a short term apparent worsening of some symptoms.

idea to get into the dive planning habit as soon as possible. Longer and deeper dives may well create nitrogen tissue loadings that require quite long and slow ascents to allow the excess gas to be released at a safe rate. It is usually easiest to manage such ascents by including a definite halt at a particular depth. These are referred to as 'staged' decompression stops and are usually performed at 3m or 6m for times laid down in the decompression tables. Dives which require such stops need more advanced skills and are to be avoided until such knowledge and experience is attained. You need also to be aware that as all dives involve an off-gassing phase at the surface, all dives must be considered as requiring decompression. This can have an effect on subsequent dives, because if the surface interval between the dives is short, the body tissues will carry a higher nitrogen load than normal when the next dive is started. This means that higher nitrogen loads will be achieved more quickly. In turn, this could result in a second dive that alone would not require decompression stops in the water, but because of the nitrogen tissue loadings from the previous dive *will* require decompression stops. Again, careful planning with decompression tables and guidance from a

dive computer can avoid such situations. Bearing this in mind, if you are diving more than once on the same day it is good practice to do your deeper dives first.

Even when a decompression table or dive computer indicates it is unnecessary, many divers will still include a precautionary stop at 6m or 3m as part of their ascent procedure, especially following repetitive, long or deep dives. This usually lasts for between one and three minutes and, as long as this is properly planned as part of the dive, is good practice. Given the correct environmental circumstances it helps promote slow ascent rates and good buoyancy control.

As it can take many hours for the body to wash out all the excess nitrogen, we need to be aware of other circumstances where higher than normal tissue saturations might be a problem. These will essentially be decompression situations, such as ascending to lower than normal atmospheric pressures by ascending hills or flying in an aircraft. Exposing your body to lower ambient pressure while your tissues are still off-gassing from a dive can create the same conditions as a too rapid ascent and so result in DCI.

Decompression tables and dive computers can provide information on precisely how long a surface interval is required, but a safe guideline is to allow 24 hours between diving and subsequently flying.

Nitrogen and narcosis

Another consequence of breathing nitrogen at increased pressure is its strange narcotic effect. As with decompression this is an effect which should not concern you during the early stages of your diving, because it is depth-related. As the partial pressure of the inhaled nitrogen increases with depth so does the narcosis. The effects experienced seem very similar to those produced by alcohol and generally become noticeable to the diver at depths greater than 30m. In this zone divers experience slowed reactions often coupled with either euphoric or depressive feelings. The narcosis disappears immediately the ambient pressure is reduced, so any problems caused by nitrogen narcosis can easily be resolved by ascending to shallower depths.

Cold and heat

Diving activities obviously involve water, generally either the sea or other stretches of open water such as lakes or rivers. The temperature of those waters is of great importance for divers. Our bodies function most efficiently at a constant temperature of 37°C and our circulatory system is used to keep our vital organs at that temperature. We are accustomed to being surrounded by air and we use clothing to help us cope with changes in air temperature. Even so, some changes, especially extremes, of temperature invoke automatic responses from our bodies to maintain that vital inner core temperature at its ideal level. If we are too hot we start to perspire and the blood flow to our skin increases, allowing it to be cooled by the evaporation of the sweat. If we are too cold then blood flow to the skin and eventually to the extremities such as fingers and toes is reduced to minimise heat lost by the circulating bloodstream. Living as we do, surrounded by the atmosphere, means that our bodies are adapted to the relatively poor heat-conducting properties of air. When immersed in water we are in an environment that conducts heat some 25 times faster than air, so heat loss is potentially a big problem. We would rarely find water at temperatures higher than 35°C to dive in, temperatures between 4°C and 32°C form the normal range met by divers, so all diving

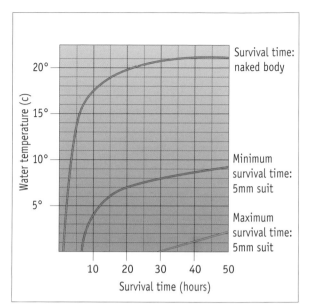

Human survival time when exposed to water

Cold and heat

Advanced symptoms of hypothermia require a slow warming of the casualty

involves heat loss to some extent. In tropical waters fairly lengthy dives can be enjoyed with minimal thermal protection, but temperate waters require progressively more adequate protection as the temperature drops.

If the core temperature drops below 35°C and the first defence of reducing surface blood flow does not rectify the situation, the body starts involuntary physical activity or shivering. This muscular activity increases metabolic rate, with a heating effect on the blood. The withdrawal of the blood from the surface capillaries and the extremities means that the blood volume in the inner core is increased. In turn, this will increase blood pressure and trigger increased urine production. If this muscular activity is unsuccessful and the core temperature falls to below 35°C, the casualty is said to be suffering from hypothermia. In this state the metabolic rate reduces, muscle stiffness appears, respiration and heartbeat slow down and blood pressure starts to fall. Thought processes also slow down and confusion can set in. With even lower core temperatures, between 30°C and 25°C, irregular breathing and heartbeat occur with unconsciousness and eventually death.

If cooling happens very rapidly there have been cases of successful reanimation even after prolonged immersion in cold water, but this is rare.

Bodies without thermal protection in 4°C water can suffer unconsciousness and death in a matter of minutes, and even in 15°C water, usual survival times are no more than five hours. Prevention is always better than cure and diving equipment such as a wetsuit or drysuit suitable for the conditions will avoid hypothermic problems while diving. We should also not forget that cooling also takes place out of the water. Wind or airflow due to transportation in a speeding boat also has a big cooling (wind-chill) effect, especially on a damp body. Protection from such effects by means of windproof clothing can be important, both before and after a dive. Recognition of the early symptoms of uncontrolled shivering and withdrawal into oneself should also indicate that immediate steps should be taken to prevent further heat loss. Treating advanced symptoms requires expert medical help and a slow rewarming of the casualty. Sudden warming from a hot drink can cause relaxation of the body's surface capillaries allowing blood from the core to be rapidly cooled and thus worsening the condition. Additionally the sudden lowering of core blood volume, and therefore blood pressure can result in severe shock and even death. Alcoholic drinks have similar effects and must not be given to people suffering serious heat loss.

One final cold-water problem is that of hydrocution. This condition is essentially a form of thermal shock and can occur when someone, usually quite hot, is suddenly immersed in cold water, typically diving into a cold lake on a hot day just to cool down. In these circumstances the thermal shock can be sufficient to stop the heart beating, with death from drowning being an added danger.

The opposite of hypothermia is excessive heating or hyperthermia. This can occur when the body cannot achieve enough of a cooling effect through perspiration and the core temperature rises too much. While not normally a problem during diving, it is something to guard against during related surface activities, particularly on open boats. Make sure that there is an adequate supply of cool drinks and shade or skin cover.

Medical conditions and diving

We have seen that respiration and circulation are both affected by diving, so it is important that divers have no existing medical conditions which could have an adverse effect on these life-sustaining systems. This also means that drugs, particularly those which could affect either the respiratory or circulatory systems, should not be used while diving without prior expert medical advice. Of course, diving under the influence of any narcotic drug or alcohol is extremely unwise and irresponsible, as it is potentially dangerous for both the affected divers and their buddies.

Asthma sufferers should seek expert medical opinion before participating in diving activities. As the symptoms experienced by diabetics and the symptoms associated with some diving problems can often be confused, diabetes is another condition needing expert opinion. Training agencies have slightly differing policies on exactly what comprises a definite exclusion from diving on medical grounds.

Of the more transitory medical conditions which can affect would-be divers, seasickness must be high on the list. The best advice has to be avoidance by traditional methods such as fresh air and keeping your vision fixed as much as possible on stable objects such as the horizon – along with a healthy lifestyle the night before! Drugs to alleviate motion sickness should be viewed with caution as they may cause drowsiness or have other harmful side effects when underwater – the brand Stugeron is generally accepted as having minimal adverse side effects. Many divers find mechanical treatments such as wrist pressure-point bands helpful. Chewing root ginger may also relieve symptoms. Sufferers are also often helped by diving as soon as possible when the boat reaches the dive site or, if conditions allow, having a short swim before preparing to dive. If the diver is particularly unwell the dive should not be undertaken. Vomiting underwater is potentially dangerous, and training to cope with such problems is difficult and probably unpopular to conduct. Fortunately, much diving takes place from boats that provide reasonably stable platforms and in fairly calm conditions. □

Fresh air and keeping your vision fixed on the horizon may help to alleviate seasickness

Chapter five
Equipment

Diving skills are, of course, a necessary and important part of your training, but without the right equipment, all the skills you have learned are wasted. Since the introduction of the aqualung, diving equipment has developed in leaps and bounds. Extremely sophisticated equipment is now available to the recreational diver at competitive prices, and there is a wide range of kit on offer. Whether you are buying the basic mask, fins and snorkel or investing in a regulator and drysuit, you should make sure that the equipment you purchase is right for the type of diving that you will be doing and that you have a basic understanding of how your equipment works.

Equipment
Instruments

Contents and depth gauge instruments

Depth gauges

The measurement of depth and time is crucial to the safety of every dive. Relying on instruments worn by someone who is diving with you is not ideal, so you need to decide fairly early on what equipment you want to buy. In the past, there was only one choice – you had to carry a waterproof diving watch and a depth gauge to track time and maximum depth in order to calculate decompression requirements. Today this function is better resolved by the use of a dive computer. Early mechanical depth gauges were notoriously inaccurate, with readings often between 3m and 4m adrift. Modern digital devices generally have a high degree of accuracy and are temperature-compensated to give reliable depth recording.

It is possible to buy digital depth gauges, but the incorporation of decompression calculation and time measurement adds so little to the cost of the device that by the time you have added the cost of a dive watch, the saving is insignificant.

Watches

Dive watches come in two basic forms – the traditional analogue type with a calibrated bezel used to measure the dive duration, and the digital type, which is essentially a sophisticated waterproof stopwatch performing the same function. There is no doubt that the heavy analogue diver's watch is much more of an eye-catcher in the local bar, but with the best will in the world it is not easy to read dive times from the bezel to anything like the accuracy of a digital watch or dive computer. Many divers have failed to accurately time their dives because they have either forgotten to correctly align the bezel at the start of the dive or have accidentally rotated it during the dive. Of course, forgetting to start a digital instrument can also result in inaccurate time measuring, but most modern dive computers are pressure-triggered and start automatically at the beginning of the dive. Analogue watches often have luminous faces, bezels and pointer markings to make them more readable in poor visibility.

In order to be read easily, digital instruments often need back lighting, and in the smaller models this can considerably shorten battery life. Indeed, digital watches with small characters can be quite difficult to read in poor underwater lighting. If budget is the prime consideration then modern dive computers are the most accurate instruments available to divers and, while seemingly the higher cost solution, are probably the most sensible investment. If you do use an analogue dive watch, don't forget to set it when your dive begins!

A traditional analogue dive watch with calibrated bezel

Computers

Dive computers come in many shapes and sizes, ranging from instruments not much larger than traditional dive watches, to full featured devices that even measure cylinder air pressure. Dive computers basically consist of an accurate internal clock and a sensitive pressure transducer which provide inputs to a microprocessor. This in turn uses a stored program, or algorithm, to compute the pressure exposure of the wearer and to calculate the resulting decompression requirements. A small screen is used to display values such as elapsed dive time, current depth, maximum depth, remaining time for a direct ascent to the surface, and times and depths of decompression stops if required. Most models will also provide audible and visual warnings should ascent rates become too rapid. There is often a choice of a wrist-mounted models or computers which are mounted in a console, together with the contents gauge on the end of a high-pressure hose from the regulator first stage.

A digital dive watch

The wrist-mounted type has the advantage of being easier to carry and so can monitor all the changes of pressure, including atmospheric pressure, that you experience which could have a bearing on your decompression requirements. Some divers consider these computers to be bulky encumbrances on the wrist. Others prefer the computer is located so that it can be read even while the hand is being used for something else, especially in ascent monitoring. The console-mounted model usually requires a hand to hold it while it is being read and some consider it a disadvantage that, attached to the regulator, it tends to travel in the diving equipment bag rather than in personal hand baggage.

The smallest wrist-mounted models do overcome the problem of bulk, but at the expense of display size. This can mean smaller display character size, the need for information to be displayed sequentially, and often, shorter battery life, as the batteries are also smaller.

As well as these essential decompression functions, many dive computers automatically log parameters, such as depth and time, at

Computers

A wrist-mounted computer

A small watch-style computer

A console-mounted computer

regular intervals so that a profile of the dive can be read back following the dive. A historic record of dives is stored and these figures can often be transferred to a personal computer for further record keeping and even graphical dive-profile display. Even factors such as ascent speed violations can be recovered! The most sophisticated models can monitor cylinder air pressure and therefore deduce air-consumption rates and predict air duration, even predicting whether or not you have sufficient air for the decompression needs it has computed. Top-of-the-range dive computers will also cater for more complex breathing gas mixtures other than air – but that's another story for advanced divers.

Thermometers

One further instrument that many divers like to carry is an underwater thermometer, and some digital watches and most computers incorporate water temperature measurement. It is worth noting that most countries use the metric system and use instruments calibrated in metres, bar and °C. However, in the USA and areas dominated by the USA, the imperial system is still used, so instruments are calibrated in feet, pounds per square inch (psi) and °F.

Knives

Traditionally, divers always carry a fearsome looking diver's knife, and most experienced divers feel quite exposed if they submerge without one. Contrary to popular belief this item is not for defence against dangerous underwater creatures, but is to protect against the dangers imposed by man-made pollution. Being snagged on abandoned or broken fishing lines and nets can be a potential problem, especially when diving some shipwrecks. In these circumstances a good knife with a serrated line-cutting blade can be a vital piece of equipment. A similarly equipped buddy is equally vital. Blades are generally stainless steel to survive the adverse underwater environment, but the best stainless steel is very difficult to keep sharp. This means that lower-grade steel is often preferable, so make sure knives are well rinsed and dried following the dive. Knives can be found in a variety of styles and sizes and are worn sheathed on the outside or inside of the calf, thigh, upper or lower arm, or

A regulator second stage mouthpiece

A regulator first stage

carried in a BC pouch or pocket. The choice of position should be based on accessibility when needed, risk of entanglement and to ensure the knife is not likely to be lost while diving.

Regulators

A key item of diving equipment, the regulator is something many divers prefer to own rather than rent. Even when travelling by air, most divers manage to squeeze it into their baggage allowance, possibly at the expense of non-diving partners. As a regulator is relatively expensive and because it plays such an important role in your underwater experience, it is useful to know something about the way it functions and the features it can offer. Your regulator has two basic tasks: to reduce the high pressure of the air in your cylinder to that of your surroundings and to deliver only the quantity of air you require. It would be simple just to reduce the pressure and have a continuous airflow at the ambient pressure, but your air supply would not last long and it would not be very comfortable to breathe from. Early regulators accomplished these two tasks in a one-

piece mechanical device that was mounted directly on the cylinder valve, inhaled air being delivered to the diver's mouthpiece, and exhaled air taken back to the regulator, via two corrugated flexible tubes.

Some of these twin-hose regulators accomplished the pressure reduction in a single stage. Later, more sophisticated models employed two pressure-reduction stages for finer control.

As regulator engineering evolved, a further type of two-stage regulator was developed, which involved physically separating these two pressure-reduction stages. The first stage continued to be mounted on the cylinder valve, while the second stage was incorporated with the mouthpiece. The first or high-pressure stage reduced the pressure to around 10 bar higher than ambient pressure and this intermediate/medium-pressure air was fed through a robust but slimmer, flexible hose to the second stage. As the diver's exhaled air could be exhausted directly from the combined mouthpiece and second stage, this type of regulator became known as a single-hose regulator, and currently dominates the recreational diving market.

It is obviously very useful to have some idea of the amount of air available from the dive cylinder at all

A scuba unit with regulator attached

stages of the dive. For this reason, contents gauges have been developed specifically for diving use. The contents gauge needs to be visible to the diver during the dive and so is connected via a flexible high-pressure hose of suitable length to the high-pressure side of the regulator first stage. By this means the diver can monitor his or her air consumption as the dive progresses, and ensure the ascent begins with an appropriate amount of air (safety reserve) remaining. Most countries use contents gauges that are calibrated in bar, but in the USA contents gauges may be calibrated in psi.

Although the principal function of the regulator is to provide breathing air to the diver, other equipment has evolved that can also make use of air from the diver's cylinder. It was long recognised that some form of emergency buoyancy to support the diver at the surface was highly desirable. Initially, life jackets of the type provided in aircraft were used, being capable of oral or small CO_2 cartridge inflation and really only usable once at the surface. These devices gradually evolved to become adjustable buoyancy life jackets (ABLJs) and then the sophisticated buoyancy compensators (BCs) so popular today. It was soon realised that oral inflation of a buoyancy device while underwater was a complex and risky procedure, so both ABLJs and BCs were provided with a system of inflation taken directly from the regulator. Concurrently, divers in cooler waters were adopting the modern version of the drysuit, which also required an inflation system to keep the insulating air within the suit at a constant volume as the diver descended. This air could also be most conveniently supplied from the regulator, so regulators began to be produced with multiple outlets or ports, incorporated in the first stage, supplying medium-pressure air to the regulator second stage, the BC and, if worn, the drysuit.

Another development in equipment was the adoption of a further regulator second stage to provide an emergency or alternate air supply (AAS) to the dive buddy, should problems arise with their breathing system. The AAS could also serve as a breathing source for the provider in the unlikely event of problems with their own second stage. For this reason, it is common for regulator first stages to be provided with at least four medium-pressure ports and at least one high-pressure port.

The second stage is the mouthpiece through which a diver breathes. The yellow-coloured octopus is used as an alternate air source

Regulators

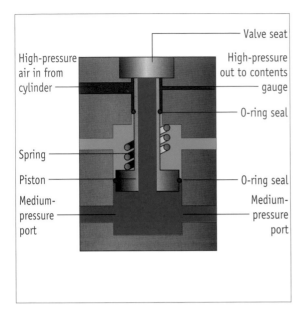

Labels on diagram:
- Valve seat
- High-pressure air in from cylinder
- High-pressure out to contents gauge
- O-ring seal
- Spring
- Piston
- O-ring seal
- Medium-pressure port
- Medium-pressure port

Balanced piston regulator first stage
If air is taken from the medium-pressure chamber (by breathing in, BC inflation, etc), the pressure is lowered, allowing the spring and surrounding water pressure to push the piston away from the valve seat. This allows high-pressure air from the cylinder to flow through the central hole in the piston into the medium-pressure chamber. Once the medium pressure has risen sufficiently to balance the spring and water pressure, the piston will again close onto the valve seat, cutting the air flow.

How does the regulator work?

The first stage of the regulator has to allow high-pressure air to flow from the dive cylinder into the inter-stage or medium-pressure hose until the pressure in the hose is some eight to ten bar above ambient pressure. It then has to close off the flow until air is drawn from the medium-pressure hose. This can be achieved using a valve controlled by means of a diaphragm or piston that is exposed on one side to the cylinder high-pressure air and on the other side to the surrounding water pressure. The valve is held open by an adjustable spring that is arranged to add to the water pressure by an amount equal to the desired inter-stage pressure. This means that the valve will open whenever the diver inhales, or when medium-pressure air is drawn off to inflate the BC or drysuit, or when the diver descends, so increasing the surrounding water pressure. Air will then flow from the cylinder until the medium-pressure level is re-established, so closing the valve and shutting off the air flow.

A further stage of pressure reduction is then required. This is to lower the inter-stage-pressure air from approximately 10 bar above ambient down to the ambient pressure – allowing the diver to inhale normally. This is the work of the second stage, which generally has a diaphragm sensing the ambient water pressure on one side while the other side is exposed to the pressure of the air in the diver's open breathing passages. If this pressure is greater than ambient pressure, ie when exhaling, the exhaust valve will open and air will bubble out until a balance is reached. On the other hand, when this pressure is lower than ambient pressure, ie when inhaling, the diaphragm will be deflected, opening the inlet valve and so allowing medium-pressure air to flow until the pressure is equalised. It will also be possible to manually depress the second-stage diaphragm, thus opening the valve and causing air to flow into the mouthpiece. This is done by pushing the purge button and can be used to clear water from the mouthpiece as it is being replaced in the mouth, if it has been flooded by removal underwater. A few models also include a manual sensitivity control, usually a knob that can be rotated to provide fine control of the pressure that triggers the opening of the second-stage valve.

This is a fairly basic description of the operation of a device that has evolved as a quite sophisticated piece of engineering. Using modern materials and clever mechanical design, regulators are able to supply the diver with air at a flow rate which caters for periods of extreme exertion, irrespective of the pressure level in the dive cylinder. This air will be supplied with a minimal increase in breathing effort so, to all intents and purposes, breathing from the regulator underwater is hardly different to normal surface breathing. To maintain the regulator at its peak performance it will need regularly servicing, at least annually. This should be performed by a trained and competent technician who has access to any special tools that may be required, as well as manufacturer-approved replacement parts.

Alternate air sources

As the buddy diver is the prime source of assistance underwater, it is logical that techniques have developed which rely on the buddy as an alternate source of breathing air. Initially this involved the complex procedure of the two divers sharing one second stage between them. The advent of buoyancy devices such as the ABLJ and BC saw techniques and equipment develop, enabling the oral-inflation hose to double as a rather primitive emergency breathing system. Some fairly sophisticated devices have been developed which allow the oral-inflation device to serve the dual purpose of additional second stage and BC inflation/deflation control. A much more satisfactory development has been the near universal adoption of the 'octopus' rig, in its simplest form an additional second stage connected to the regulator first stage. Called an octopus because of the multiplicity of hoses emanating from the first stage, this is the equipment configuration understood by most divers to form an AAS. Because the main purpose of this extra second stage is to provide air to a buddy, it usually has a longer medium-pressure hose, and both hose and mouthpiece are often a bright yellow colour for easy location.

The extra-long hose allows the buddy pair to position themselves more comfortably when sharing air and completing the subsequent ascent. Some thought has to be given to the positioning of the AAS and its hose, make sure it is not in danger of snagging yet is immediately accessible. The hose can often be tucked into special BC sheathing, and special 'snatch' clips have been developed to secure the mouthpiece.

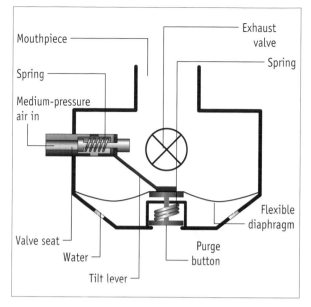

Regulator piston second stage

If air is breathed through the mouthpiece, the ambient water pressure will push the diaphragm inwards and the tilt lever will lift the piston from the valve seat, allowing medium-pressure air into the chamber. Once air is no longer being breathed from the chamber, the pressure will balance and push the diaphragm outwards, so allowing the tilt lever to shut off the air flow. The purge button allows manual override to force the valve open and allow air into the chamber. Exhaled air escapes through the exhaust valve. Because the piston opens in the direction of air flow, the design of the second stage is referred to as a 'downstream-type'.

The dive cylinder

The purge button allows a diver to clear air from the mouthpiece

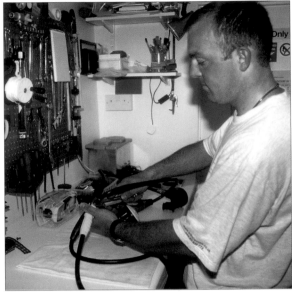

Regulators need frequent servicing

It is very important that the main second stage and the AAS are compatible types of regulator. Individuals involved in more advanced diving often, for the sake of more security, carry a small 'pony' cylinder with its own totally independent regulator. This can then act as an emergency source of air for a buddy or provide a self-contained solution for the carrier.

Dive cylinders

Also referred to as a 'tank' or 'bottle', the dive cylinder is a vital and highly specialised part of the diver's equipment. Made from either aluminium or steel, it is designed to cope with the very high pressures needed to compress the volume of air required during your dive. The amount of air a cylinder can provide is determined by two important characteristics – its working pressure and its capacity. Capacity is the amount of air it will contain at normal atmospheric pressure, or the amount of water you could pour into it. The working pressure is the maximum pressure to which it should be filled, typically in the 200 to 300-bar region. Measured in bar it can give you a simple mental image of how much air you have – a cylinder filled to

200 bar would be the equivalent of 200 cylinders at 1 bar. Cylinder capacities are normally 10 or 12 litres, with 15 and 18 litres not uncommon. Divers also use twin cylinders to provide additional capacity for more advanced diving.

The capacity and working pressure can be checked – this information is stamped around the neck of the cylinder, along with the test pressure, the cylinder weight and date of manufacture and last test. All high-pressure cylinders are made to very exacting specifications and are required to undergo periodic tests to ensure they still meet that specification. If the cylinder passes its test, the test date is stamped on the cylinder. If it does not, the cylinder has to be rendered unusable. Compressor operators are not allowed to fill cylinders that do not have a valid test date stamp. Many test regimes demand an annual internal and external visual check, backed up by less frequent hydraulic test, both of which should be conducted by a competent technician. A full or 'charged' cylinder is at around 100 times the pressure of a car tyre and could be extremely dangerous if the energy stored in this compressed gas were to be released explosively.

Treat dive cylinders with care, avoiding surface

A selection of cylinders

damage that can promote corrosion and situations that could produce overheating or impacts that could damage the cylinder valve.

Some 10 and 12-litre cylinders have a working pressure of 207 bar. Filled to that pressure they would provide 2,070 or 2,484 litres respectively. A fill of 232 bar is another common standard, giving theoretical filled volumes of 2,320 and 2,784 litres. When cylinders are filled, the action of compressing air will raise the temperature to above normal. As the air and cylinder gradually cool down, or upon cooling by immersing the cylinder in the sea, the internal pressure will fall a little, so you will often start the dive with pressure readings of, say, 200 bar or 220 bar, depending on the initial charged cylinder pressure and the degree of cooling. In these cases the actual air available from a 12-litre cylinder will be 2,400 or 2,640 litres, a fall of some five per cent after cooling. It is good practice to determine the amount of air available and, knowing your typical air consumption, deduce whether or not you have sufficient air for your dive, together with an appropriate reserve.

Cylinder valves

DIN threaded fitting

A-clamp fitting

Cylinder valves

The cylinder valve is screwed into the neck of the cylinder and provides an attachment for the regulator, as well as allowing the air supply to be turned on and off. The regulator is seated against the valve outlet by means of either an A-clamp yoke fitting or a DIN threaded ring fitting. A-clamp fittings are fairly simple to use and robust in service, however they are not very streamlined and can be snagged on any lines or nets encountered underwater. When assembling make sure the regulator is squarely seated on the O-ring seal before tightening the yoke screw into its locating recess. Care must be taken not to cross-thread DIN fittings and care must be taken not to damage the screw by 'cross-threading'.

As scuba diving has evolved, in order to carry more and more breathing gas, cylinders have been developed with ever higher working pressures. With pressures of more than 250 bar many feel the engineering limits of the current A-clamp have been reached and higher pressures will see a move to the DIN screw fitting. This is already popular for use with divers wishing to extend their range using twinned cylinders and extra side-slung cylinders. Here, besides the high working pressures, the advantages of the more streamlined form are appreciated and outweigh the increased complexity involved in assembling the screw fitting. DIN fittings are more difficult to clean and suffer a risk of thread damage demanding greater care in the rough and tumble of the normal diving environment. The seal between the valve and regulator is achieved by means of an O-ring, and care should be taken when assembling the scuba set to make sure that the cylinder valve seat, O-ring and regulator are all free from dirt. This is particularly important in the case of DIN fittings, where dust and sand can cause potentially dangerous wear of the thread over time. Inspect the O-ring carefully for wear or damage and if necessary replace it, under pressure leaking and bursting O-rings can have dramatic effects. Earlier cylinder valves were difficult to operate and tended to have slight leaks if opened completely, so a habit of fully opening the valve, then turning it back half a turn was common practice. Modern balanced valves are much improved and, provided excessive force is not used, do not need this precaution. Indeed, there is much less chance of confusion if cylinder valves are always either fully open or fully closed, and equipment checking is much simpler. The internal valve seals and parts subject to wear are normally inspected and, if necessary, changed at the same time as the cylinder is inspected.

A cylinder being filled with air

Compressors

Diving cylinders are not filled with oxygen (as some misinformed people believe), but usually contain compressed air. This air is taken from the atmosphere, filtered and then pumped at very high pressure into the diving cylinder by a special compressor. It is important that the air you are using is as free from pollutants as possible, because the action of compression means the subsequent partial pressure of any contaminants will be significantly raised. Air-filling stations need to take care that traffic fumes and boat engine exhausts do not pollute the air intake. If the compressor is powered by a combustion engine, that exhaust must be well separated from the air intake, and wind direction must always be taken into account during filling operations. To reach the very high pressures required by divers, the compressor generally has three or four stages, pumping to progressively higher pressures. Between each stage the air is cooled and filtered. After leaving the final stage, the air is passed through a final filter to ensure it is sufficiently free of any lubricating oil mist or excess water vapour. It is important that the components of this filter and the compressor lubricating oil are changed in line with manufacturers' recommendations to maintain the air purity. The quality of the compressed air should be regularly sampled and tested for purity. Besides filling directly from the compressor, some filling stations maintain a reservoir system of large storage cylinders known as a 'bank'. This can enable a large number of diving cylinders to be filled fairly quickly and the compressor used to support this process can then be used to top up the air bank afterwards. Working with high-pressure air and the associated compressors requires special training. This is an activity best left to those with that training and a proper understanding of the necessary safety procedures.

A modern buoyancy compensator

Buoyancy compensators

The first real buoyancy compensation device was in the style of a horse collar and could be inflated by using a small high-pressure air cylinder or an oral inflation tube. This emergency cylinder, of between 0.4 and 0.6 litres, had to be charged from the dive cylinder before each dive. Initially it was conceived as surface life jacket and a kind of underwater parachute. However, being filled directly from a high-pressure source and having fairly crude dump valves made buoyancy control during an ascent rather problematic. In the early days many people thought the device could be used as an emergency breathing system, but breathing from the jacket demanded considerable skill and was not a viable option in a real emergency. It wasn't until the adoption of the medium-pressure direct-feed inflation system (power inflator) that a practical adjustable buoyancy life jacket (ABLJ) system was born. Along with this development there also evolved the inflatable waistcoat-style of buoyancy device, commonly referred to as a stab (stabiliser) jacket.

The stab jacket had two main advantages over the ABLJ – it was more comfortable to wear and it provided a simpler method of attaching the dive cylinder to the diver. Against that, it suffered the disadvantage that it was no longer practical for the user to remove the cylinder without also removing their buoyancy aid. There were also concerns that an unconscious wearer could be left in a face-down position when floating at the surface, but incident analysis has shown that this is not a problem. History has shown that the advantages outweigh the disadvantages. Subsequently there have been many developments to the early waistcoat design, many concerned by adding extra functionality such as pockets and clips. Others have been more basic, such as the 'wings'-style that shifts the main buoyancy to the rear of the diver to give a face-down underwater swimming position.

There are several key functions that the majority of divers demand from their buoyancy compensators: surface flotation, buoyancy adjustment and equipment support.

The functions of surface support and buoyancy adjustment are necessarily interlinked, and some compromise has to be made where their ideals conflict. Buoyancy compensation devices do not work exactly like a life jacket because such a device demands permanent buoyancy, and that would make it difficult for the wearer to swim underwater. Ideally a life jacket

An old-fashioned horse collar-style buoyancy compensation device

Buoyancy compensators

Oral inflation hoses often include dump valves

The inflator hose allows air to be introduced into the BC

will always bring an unconscious wearer into a face-up position and support the head as high as possible above the surface. Unfortunately, buoyancy arranged in this manner does not allow the diver to adopt a comfortable position when underwater. Fortunately, arranging the buoyancy to suit divers does not appear to have any adverse effect on the safety of the diver on the surface.

To achieve buoyancy changes, methods are needed to increase and decrease the overall volume of water displaced by the diver and his equipment. Assuming that the volume of the diver and the rest of the equipment remain constant, this can be achieved by simply changing the volume of the BC.

Its volume can be increased by inflating it, and this is best performed by a direct-feed hose from a medium-pressure port on the regulator first stage. The hose incorporates a quick connect/release coupling attaching it to the mouthpiece end of the BC oral-inflation tube. This is where a push-button controlled valve is placed, allowing the user to control when and how much air is admitted to the BC. Should the inflator hose become detached from the BC the coupling is automatically shut off so that there is no

loss of air from the diver's cylinder. However, this means there is no obvious sign this has happened, so take care to include a pre-dive check on the security of the coupling. Once under pressure, it is very unlikely that the inflator hose will become accidentally disconnected. Normal increases in buoyancy are made by briefly depressing the inflation button, allowing controlled amounts of air into the BC. More rarely, BCs have an additional, small, high-pressure cylinder as an alternative inflation system.

A second push-button that operates a vent valve is also placed at the mouthpiece end of the oral inflation tube. In order to completely vent air from the BC, the tube is held above the shoulder while this button is operated. The vent valve is not very large, so air is vented relatively slowly and consequent buoyancy changes are easy to control. Most BCs are also fitted with one or more 'dump' valves. These are larger sized valves that, when opened, allow a large volume of air to rapidly exhaust from the BC. This will produce the rapid loss of buoyancy that may be appropriate should too much buoyancy be leading to an out-of-control ascent. Some dump valves are fitted at the upper shoulder on the opposite side to the oral inflation tube attachment. A second dump valve may be fitted to the lower back section in order to dump air when in a head-down attitude. Most dump valves are operated by pulling a toggle on a short lanyard attached directly to the valve, although sometimes the lanyard is routed through a guide to a more accessible position. Some models have a dump valve incorporated in the oral inflation tube. As it is corrugated, it can be extended by pulling, and this stretching is used to operate a dump valve built in to the tube shoulder attachment. Should your equipment require this method of operation, it should be carefully explained to dive buddies who might be more familiar with other inflation/deflation systems. Most BCs will have one or two storage pouches or pockets and possibly a number of D-ring attachment points to enable various items of ancillary equipment – such as torches – to be carried.

The BC will have two attachment systems, one to fasten the dive cylinder to the jacket and one to fasten the jacket to the diver. The cylinder is usually held in place by a strap with a cam-action buckle that can be adjusted to cope with cylinders of different diameters. There may be a second cylinder strap for added security, but take great care to ensure the cylinder is tightly secured and check that it cannot slide out of the harness. In positioning the cylinder, be careful not to place it too high in the harness to avoid hitting your head on the regulator or cylinder valve, especially when leaning back for mask clearing! Once the cylinder and BC are assembled, fit the regulator and connect the BC inflation hose. The scuba unit can then be pressurised and tested.

The scuba unit can either be placed on a conveniently raised surface or lifted to the right height by your buddy to help you slip into the BC. There are a wide variety of methods of fitting the BC to the diver. The arm openings may have two adjustable straps with quick-release snap buckles. If the BC does have these adjustable shoulder straps, it is common to set them to maximum length for ease in putting on the scuba unit. The ends of the shoulder straps can then be pulled down tight, assuring a comfortable but snug fit. There will probably be a broad, cummerbund-style waistband that has Velcro fastening, again to ensure a snug and comfortable fit. This is often backed up by a webbing strap with an adjustable snap-fit buckle, and possibly another similar strap higher up across the chest. Ensure that these straps are fully tight only when the BC is fully inflated. Once it is in

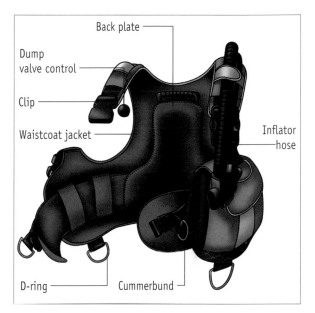

A buoyancy compensator

Buoyancy compensators

The cylinder is attached to the back of the BC and with the aid of a buddy can easily be slipped on

place, complete your buddy checks and make sure your AAS, contents gauge and hoses are all tidy and secured in place ready to commence the dive.

Taking off the scuba unit is simply a reverse of putting it on. First, detach any chest and waist straps, followed by the cummerbund. Release or free one arm, usually on the opposite side to that of your regulator second stage, and carefully shrug off the BC. Following this procedure when taking off kit in the water means removing the regulator from your mouth can be the final manoeuvre.

Many divers like to record their end-of-dive cylinder pressure to provide air-consumption data. Close the cylinder valve and completely depressurise the system by depressing the purge button of either your main second stage or AAS. Check depressurisation is complete by observing the contents gauge before detaching the regulator from the BC and cylinder. Fit the regulator dust cap to prevent dirt and water entering the regulator first stage.

Note that most BCs can now be obtained in a range of sizes, and your diving will be much more enjoyable in equipment that fits you securely. In choosing the most suitable model, test its fit – both deflated and fully inflated – and bear in mind the rest of the equipment you will be using with it. If you dive with a drysuit, check that suit inflation and deflation points are freely accessible.

Full-length wetsuits

A shortie wetsuit

Protective clothing: wetsuits

Water conducts heat some 25 times faster than air, so we need to prevent the layer of water warmed by our bodies from washing away and being replaced by cooler water. The wetsuit achieves this by being tailored from a stretchy, flexible material that can thus be close-fitting and trap just a thin layer of water in contact with the body. This water soon warms and provides us with a comfortable diving environment. To help the water stay warm, the suit is made from neoprene foam, a synthetic rubber made to be a poor heat conductor by being filled with small gas bubbles. Manufacturers use neoprene of various thickness, from 2mm to 9mm, to make wetsuits for use in various water temperatures. Bear in mind that, although flexible, considerable effort is required to move in thicker suits and swimming in a 9mm suit for any length of time can be quite tiring.

To make dressing easier and wearing them more comfortable, the inside surface of the neoprene is often lined with a layer of nylon stretch fabric.

The exterior surface is also often finished in a similar manner to increase the durability of the suit, and for the same reason protective pads are placed over the knee sections. Early suits were cut to simple patterns and the pieces were simply glued together. Today's double-lined suits are both glued and stitched, often employing a special stitching that does not pierce the neoprene, so avoiding water-flow through the seams.

One effect of wearing a suit containing bubbles of gas is the inherent buoyancy it provides and this must be compensated for by an equivalent increase in weight if the diver is to submerge. Once underwater there is the disadvantage that with the increase in depth and therefore pressure, so the volume of the gas bubbles in the neoprene decreases. In turn, this has the double effect of lowering the effectiveness of the thermal insulation as the water gets colder, and decreasing the buoyancy of the suit. The decrease in buoyancy can be corrected by putting air into the BC, but there is no way of making up for the insulation loss.

Drysuits

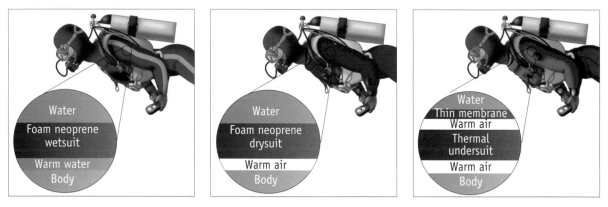

Cross-section of a neoprene wetsuit   Cross-section of a neoprene drysuit   Cross-section of a membrane drysuit

Drysuits

Bearing in mind that water is so much better at conducting heat than air, it is logical to avoid direct contact with the water and to try to maintain a 'bubble' of air round as much of the body as possible. The semi-drysuit attempts to do this by having either latex or soft, unlined neoprene seals around the wrists, neck and ankles. The ankle seals are sometimes replaced with built-in waterproof boots. In this way water is kept away from most of the body. The small volume of air trapped within the suit will compress with increasing depth but, provided the fit is fairly close and there are no significant creases, this should not prove too uncomfortable. As they are semi-dry, a small amount of water may enter these suits, but because of the seals around the wrist, neck and ankles, there will be much less of a 'flushing' effect than experienced with a wetsuit, hence better heat retention.

The next stage, in terms of thermal protection, was to make a foam neoprene suit that was as waterproof as possible and relatively loose fitting so that a layer of insulating underclothing could be worn. This underclothing insulates by trapping a layer of air between the body surface and the suit material. In order to maintain the effectiveness of this insulating layer as pressure is increased, further air needs to be introduced into the suit. This is achieved by means of a flexible hose connecting a push-button control valve on the chest of the suit to a medium-pressure port on the regulator. As the descent is made the diver can inject air into the suit to preserve a constant volume, so maintaining insulation and avoiding potential areas of squeeze. The problems of buoyancy change due to compression of the foam neoprene remain unchanged but may be compensated for by feeding a little extra air into the suit. As the diver has only one air volume to control, dive management is made much simpler and therefore safer.

As the diver ascends, the air in a drysuit will expand. To maintain constant volume and neutral buoyancy, some air will need to be let out of the suit. An 'automatic' dump valve is fitted, generally on the upper arm, allowing air to escape automatically should a preset pressure be exceeded. Depressing the valve allows the diver to dump air manually, should this be required and by screwing the valve control in or out the preset pressure may be varied. As an alternative,

Left, a neoprene drysuit; right, a membrane drysuit

some suits are fitted with a cuff dump from which air can be vented simply by raising your arm. Entry to these suits is normally made via a waterproof shoulder zip, waterproof boots are incorporated, with the wrist and neck seals are made by neoprene or latex rubber seals. Seals are usually left flat against the skin surface, but neoprene neck seals are normally folded back inside the suit. This can produce a firmer seal, with the air inside the suit pressing the seal onto the skin. However, when the seals are arranged like this over-pressurised air cannot escape by forcing the seal from the skin.

To avoid changes in buoyancy and to provide better waterproofing and tear resistance, the membrane drysuit was developed. This employs a strong

waterproof fabric for its main construction, but is otherwise very similar to the neoprene drysuit in its fittings. As the suit material has little thermal insulation value compared to foam neoprene, the undergarments play the principal role in the retention of body heat. Because the material is not compressible, as depth increases there is no inherent buoyancy loss (nor corresponding gain on ascent). This means that as depth increases there is only the compression and expansion of the insulating air within the suit to be controlled. Membrane suits are much easier to flex and so less tiring to wear, but also tend to be of loose fit. The loose fit can allow air to migrate around the suit depending upon the diver's attitude in the water, this air can lead to forces which turn the diver oddly. In

A compass is a useful navigation tool

extreme cases this can lead to air collecting around the legs and feet, creating a head-down position that can be difficult to recover from without practise, particularly if there is stretching of the boots that causes fins to pop off! Avoidance being better than cure, choose a suit that fits the body as closely as possible and ensure the air volume contained in the suit is the minimum consistent with comfort and insulation needs. This has the further advantage that less lead needs to be carried on the weight belt. Test for vertical fit by checking that you can comfortably crouch down in the suit.

While a few drysuits have attached dry hoods, most rely on a foam, neoprene hood such as those used with a wetsuit. Likewise there are dry gloves available, but most divers use thin, foam neoprene or standard work gloves, or no gloves at all should sensitivity to cold permit. To assist putting on non-lined wetsuits and the tight fitting seals of drysuits, French chalk (talcum powder) is normally sprinkled on the latex or neoprene as a lubricant. Liquid soap is sometimes used, but for comfort reasons should be avoided if there is any sand nearby!

Waterproof zips should be kept clean and lubricated if they are to be effective, coating with beeswax is recommended. Treat wrist and neck seals with particular care, especially when dressing and undressing, and avoid tearing them with sharp jewellery or fingernails.

Don't forget that a watch or computer is not very usable if it is inside your drysuit, so remember to remove it before putting on the suit and then re-fit it on the outside of the arm. Make sure the strap is long enough and can remain secure during expansion and contraction of the suit, and that winding mechanisms will not puncture delicate wrist seals.

Compasses

Many divers carry a compass specially adapted for underwater use. The compass may be wrist-mounted, included in the contents gauge console or attached to the BC, sometimes on a small navigation board. Note, there is little point in carrying this instrument as a kind of travel good luck charm – you need to study and practise navigation skills if it is to be of practical use.

Lights

To view dark crevices, see the hidden colours of deeper objects and animals, or to enjoy diving at night the diver needs to be equipped with some form of underwater lighting. This can range from the tiny pencil torches, through the hand-lantern size and on up to massive surface-supplied floodlights for filming. Most divers prefer to fit a new set of batteries prior to each dive, to minimise the risk of running out of light at a critical moment. Alternatively, some lights can be equipped with rechargeable cells and obviously this should be done just before each dive. Carrying one of the small, pencil torches on every dive is a common practice and carrying two lights on a night dive is considered prudent.

Equipment maintenance

Salt water and chlorinated swimming pool water are both highly corrosive and all equipment should be rinsed thoroughly as soon as possible following such dives, and then allowed to dry, especially if it is going to be stored for any length of time. Items such as regulators and cylinders should be serviced regularly in line with the manufacturer's recommendations. As well as rinsing and drying BCs, regular flushing out of the bladder with fresh water and a mild disinfectant is recommended by many manufacturers. Non-chromed or painted metal surfaces such as knife blades, and threaded surfaces such as torch battery housings, usually benefit from a light coating of silicone grease after rinsing and drying. Most diving equipment will have a longer life if stored in cool, dry and dark conditions. Once dry, neoprene and other rubber products should be given a light coat of talcum powder before storage. □

Chapter six

More diving skills

As your dive training progresses, your experience and confidence in your diving ability will grow. Each new skill learned, will extend your capacity to become self-reliant in the water and will allow you to accept responsibility for both yourself and others while diving. Buddy diving will increase your enjoyment of the underwater world, offering you the chance to share your experiences with another diver. It also provides each buddy with immediate assistance, if required, adding to your safety in the water.

More diving skills
Buddy diving

Buddies provide each other with companionship and safety

In the early days of diving, when 'hard hats' and surface-pumped air supplies were used, much of a diver's activities were controlled directly from the surface, to which he or she was tethered. The surface team also played a large part in the diver's security, with a fully equipped and prepared standby diver ready to enter the water to resolve any problems or rescue the diver. Today's scuba gear gives us a large degree of freedom and independence from the surface support, and this very independence means a standby diver at the surface could offer little support in the event of any difficulty. Locating a free-swimming diver, unattached to the surface, would be very

problematic. To create a safer approach to recreational diving a buddy support system has developed.

Effectively, the fully equipped standby diver is still there, but nowadays he is swimming at your side, ready to assist and help resolve any problems that might arise. In temperate waters, often with more limited visibility, it is customary to dive as a pair of divers, each diver acting as buddy to the other. In waters with greater visibility, diving in larger groups is often practised. In this case there will be a group leader, possibly assisted by a 'sheepdog' diver to help keep the group together. However, with the many underwater distractions coupled with the narrower

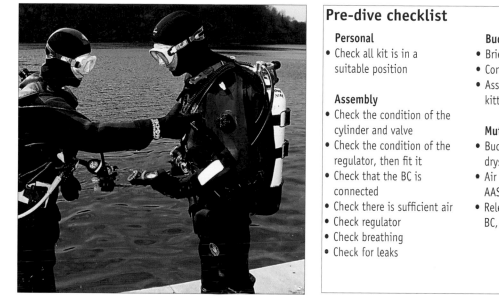

A diver familiarises himself with his buddy's equipment

Pre-dive checklist

Personal
- Check all kit is in a suitable position

Assembly
- Check the condition of the cylinder and valve
- Check the condition of the regulator, then fit it
- Check that the BC is connected
- Check there is sufficient air
- Check regulator
- Check breathing
- Check for leaks

Buddy
- Brief
- Confirm plan and signals
- Assist each other in kitting up

Mutual equipment check
- Buoyancy – hoses, BC and drysuit inflation/deflation
- Air breathing quantity, AAS
- Releases – weight belt, BC, other (drysuit etc)

Pre-dive buddy checklist

angle of vision provided by a dive mask, observing the whole group all the time is not simple. This means that within groups even in good visibility the buddy system should still be practised – by pairing off the divers – as it provides a much higher level of security.

To be a competent buddy, you should conduct a pre-dive buddy check, which has two functions – to check the correct working state of each diver's equipment and to learn how to operate your buddy's equipment. Should the circumstance arise, it could be crucial for each of you to know exactly where each other's AAS is positioned and released. Not all equipment is identical and there is considerable variety in the style and operation of BC inflation systems. Make sure you each understand how to inflate and deflate each other's equipment. Likewise, this understanding should extend to include the positioning and operation of dump valves and oral-inflation mechanisms. A number of BC systems use oral-inflation hoses that incorporate a dump-valve mechanism. When these are used for controlled deflation via the mouthpiece, be careful not to pull on the hose and activate the dump mechanism, as this could result in an uncontrolled loss of buoyancy!

It is important to understand the position, fastening and releasing of all equipment straps, buckles or other fastenings and this is particularly so with regard to the weight belt. Do not forget the connection and release of items such as drysuit hoses and the operation of drysuit inflation and deflation controls when these are worn. Simple things, such as the position of contents gauges, depth, time and decompression instruments should be noted, as well as a check that you understand how to read these instruments.

While paired with a particular buddy, you may well be diving as part of a larger group, or encounter other divers while underwater. In these circumstances it is always a good idea to be able to easily recognise your buddy. With everyone fully dressed in diving equipment and with the possibility of reduced visibility, having some key identification feature can be very useful to avoid possible separation. A careful note of distinguishing features such as mask or fin style or colour can help, but do remember colours become much harder to distinguish underwater, especially at increased depths.

A good buddy check should provide you with a complete familiarisation of your buddy's equipment.

Buddies should be familiar with the operation of one another's equipment

While you are in the early stages of gaining this habit there is a good exercise to reinforce such learning. Once you have both carried out the pre-dive buddy check, turn to face away from each other. From memory, describe to each other the position and operation of key items of equipment, which your buddy can then confirm or correct. If you dive regularly with the same buddy it is all too easy for these checks to become rather casual. Always think 'safety' and take buddy checks seriously.

Underwater

If you are to act as a team you must also ensure that you and your buddy can communicate effectively. While you have learned the basic international signal code for diving, inevitably local 'dialects' creep in. Check that you really can communicate effectively before entering the water together. Once in the water, you and your buddy are somewhat like aircraft flying in formation and need to keep in contact with one another. Obviously you need to always be within visual contact, but you should also be within a distance where you can render physical assistance should it be needed. Distances are deceptive underwater so avoid straying more than a few fin strokes apart. Think about the limited angle of vision set by a dive mask and try to maintain a position where each of you can easily glance at the other. Avoid constantly changing your relative position – the idea is to enjoy the underwater scene, not to be constantly searching for a buddy who is shooting all over the place! Monitor your own instruments and from time to time check readings with your buddy.

While awareness of your buddy should be constant, there are key times when extra vigilance is appropriate. Make sure you keep in close contact during the descent – separation is possible should one of you be slow in ear clearing, for example. This is also the case during the dive, whenever depth or direction changes occur. Air quantities are regularly checked, but key stages in the dive, such as when cylinders reach half pressure and one third pressure, are usually verified with buddies. With experience, buddy awareness should become second nature. Always remember your buddy is your safety diver and likewise you act as safety diver for your buddy. Once at the surface, stay with your buddy, mutual assistance in either getting ashore or removal of kit and passing diving gear from the

A diver signals to his buddy that his air supply is at 50 bar

water into a small boat makes diving much simpler. A big advantage of buddy diving is that, having shared the underwater experience, you can reinforce the memories by discussing the dive afterwards. For the sake of safety, avoid doing this when you surface. Keep your mask and regulator in place and wait until you are out of the water and the equipment is all tidied away and the dive really complete.

Boat diving

Purpose-built dive boats with diving platforms make entering the water extremely easy

On board, equipment is carefully stored, with fins near to the entry point and cylinders placed in racks

Boat diving

A diver's swimming range in and under the water is fairly limited, since he or she is only propelled by fin power. This means that the number and choice of dive sites available from shore access is also limited, so to reach more distant dive sites we need to use boats. Historically, divers first extended their range by using small craft, and the inflatable boat powered by an outboard engine became, and remains, very popular. It was relatively easy to transport on land to many different coastal venues and not too difficult to launch. As diving grew in popularity it became commercially viable for small fishing vessels to be made available for hire – the owners were also in possession of valuable knowledge of local tidal conditions and potentially interesting dive spots. To reach more inaccessible diving areas and to cater for extended diving expeditions, larger fishing vessels that could provide both accommodation and air-refilling facilities became available. A number of retired fishing trawlers were converted specifically to cater for this new liveaboard diving market. As the demand for boat diving has expanded, a whole spectrum of specialist purpose-built boats has also evolved, ranging from small, fast, rigid-hulled inflatable craft through to the large, day-trip dive platforms and on up to the luxury liveaboard cruisers more usually found in the tropics. In the Caribbean there are even luxury liners which have been specifically converted to cater for cruising and diving for a clientele numbering several hundred!

Such boat diving can be extremely enjoyable. In addition to the wide variety of dive sites, it is possible to kit up and enter the water exactly where we want to, and with the same exit advantages. Diving equipment is not light, so carrying it by boat can usually greatly minimise the distance you have to hand carry it. A week's cruising on a well-appointed liveaboard with an entertaining group of diving companions can provide an unsurpassable diving holiday.

To make the most of boat diving there are a few sensible habits it is well worth observing. Firstly, space is usually at a premium, so keep your personal and diving needs as simple as possible. Make sure everything you need is tidily and compactly carried in a manner that things are easily available as and when needed and that fragile objects are suitably protected. This is especially so when diving from small boats.

Boat diving has become a popular way of diving and there are now many liveaboard operators

Boat diving

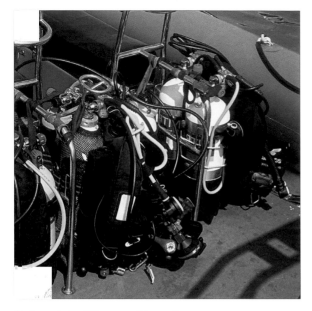

Equipment should be secured in a safe manner

Buddies perform a check prior to a boat dive

Inflatables and rigid-hulled inflatables have massive buoyancy reserves, but this is at the expense of internal space for passengers and equipment. Add to this the need to carefully place divers and gear so that their combined weight creates the correct trim for the boat and you will understand the need for efficient packing of your equipment. Experienced divers pack their dive bags so that items such as fins that are put on last are at the bottom of the bag.

BCs and regulators are stowed at the top of dive bags, so that the diver is ready to assemble the scuba set as the first task. Dive cylinders are stowed either flat on the decking or vertically in purpose-built central racking, with bags placed towards the bow.

The driver (or coxswain) will either have a centrally mounted steering console with motorcycle-style seating, or will sit on one of the side tubes if the boat is steered by an engine-mounted tiller control. Other passengers will usually be seated on the side tubes, with looped lanyards available to hold themselves in place. This lack of space also means kitting up has to be quite disciplined, often only one buddy pair kitting up at a time. Indeed, if the journey is fairly short, it is sometimes advantageous to do as much of your kitting up as possible before leaving the shore.

Kitting up should follow the same buddy principles as learned earlier, with entry being controlled by a dive marshal. Divers and propellers do not mix well so it is imperative that the engine be at least in neutral, if not stopped, before divers enter the water. Buddy pairs will frequently enter the water by backward rolls on opposite sides of the boat, in order to maintain stability within the boat.

If the dive boat is free you will probably be dropped close to a buoyed shot-line that will act as a guide down to the dive site. In this case, it is best to clear the boat as quickly as possible and rendezvous with your buddy at the shot-line buoy. This allows the boat to regain its manoeuvrability in the shortest possible time, as it cannot safely re-engage the propeller drive while there are divers free-swimming in the water close by.

Should the boat be anchored, it is usual for the divers to rendezvous at the bow before descending together, often following the descent-line down.

If you are correctly weighted and therefore neutrally buoyant you should not need to pull on the descent-line – simply loop a finger and thumb around it and use it as a guide.

Before divers enter the water the boat engine should be in neutral

Divers hold on to a line at the surface

Coming back to the boat at the end of the dive is more or less a reverse of the entry technique. If you have ascended a shot-line and have a mobile cover boat on the surface, be careful to remain at the shot line buoy while making contact with the boat-cover party. The boat should then approach, putting the engine in neutral before closing up on the divers. Wait until signalled that it is safe to swim to the boat and carry out the exit from the water described above. If anchored, simply ascend via the anchor-line then assist your buddy to remove weight belt and scuba set – which is passed into the boat – and allow your buddy to help you in the same way. Then, in turn, each of you fully immerses beside the boat before finning vigorously upwards and pulling yourselves over the side tube into the boat. Sometimes it is better to position yourselves on either side of the boat for this stage to assist the boat's stability.

Using larger boats as diving platforms generally does provide more room for equipment stowage and kitting up, as well as providing more stability at sea. This, however, does not remove the need to be reasonably disciplined with placement of gear bags, as space will still be limited – often a larger boat equates to a larger complement of divers. Kitting up is usually more comfortable, but there is much more opportunity for disorganised divers to scatter their gear around. You will soon become unpopular if you are ready to enter the water at one end of the boat with your fins at the other and your dive mask somewhere else. Entering the water is achieved by a variety of means, often depending on the size of the boat and its original design purpose.

Fishing vessels are generally not designed to provide easy access to and from the water for their occupants. Smaller vessels are usually exited using a backward roll from a seated position on the gunwale. With larger vessels a stride entry from a standing position on the gunwale or through a port in the gunwale is most common. In these cases you will need to hold on to something, such as part of the boat rigging, to steady yourself. Purpose-built larger dive boats may also provide similar entry points for standing divers, though many also use the rear water-level diver recovery platforms as entry points.

Recovery methods into fishing vessels vary and can be quite strenuous if the vessel has a high freeboard. Simplest to use are angled, centre-spine ladders and

A centre-spine ladder makes exiting the water a relatively easy procedure

Some larger boats have purpose-built dive platforms and centre-spine ladders

it is often preferable to climb these fully kitted, with someone on the deck to assist at the top of the ladder. Conventional ladders are best ascended after taking off your fins, and if the climb is high and vertical, removal of your weight belt and even your scuba set may be advisable, as long as these can be recovered by someone on board. Those dive boats with rear sea-level platforms are the simplest to use, especially if they have a centre-spine ladder extending under the water. You simply swim onto the ladder and climb onto the platform, where fins are normally removed before climbing up onto the deck. Larger vessels can pitch and roll with the waves, so make sure you stay clear until it is time for you to board and then carefully judge your approach to avoid being hit by the hull

or caught underneath the platform. As with smaller vessels it is vital that the propeller is not engaged, so make sure you are given the signal that it is safe to approach the boat.

In all cases, remember to clear the exit point as quickly as possible to leave it free for other divers. Remove your kit with your buddy and collect and stow away all diving gear, as it is dangerous to leave it scattered around, obstructing the deck, not to mention the risk of it being lost overboard. Fresh water is a precious commodity on boats, but if there is sufficient supply it is a good idea to rinse your dive computer and photographic equipment before the salt has a chance to dry and encrust. This is particularly relevant during boat expeditions of several days or more.

Snorkelling

All sorts of animal life, including sharks, can be seen while snorkelling

Snorkel swimming

Light is the principal energy source for life in the oceans and because this energy is progressively absorbed as depth increases, it is not surprising that the shallower waters reveal the greatest abundance of marine life. Here, too, we can most easily observe the full spectrum of colours of these undersea plants and creatures. What this means is that some of the most interesting underwater sites are available with the most basic of diving equipment, a dive mask and snorkel. For efficient propulsion, fins are usually included to give us what most divers refer to as 'basic equipment'. As previously explained, your natural floating position is face-down, with the back of the

head just breaking the surface. In this position you can hang almost effortlessly, breathing gently through your snorkel and observing the underwater world through your mask. Here, you also have the enormous advantage of an unlimited supply of air.

Of course, snorkelling does not end there, you will want to dive beneath the surface to get a closer look and swim among the underwater inhabitants. Here, some basic physics comes into play. You inhale air into your lungs by tightening the diaphragm at the bottom of lungs downwards, and allowing your ribs to move outwards. These movements expand the chest cavity and so lower the air pressure in your

When snorkelling, adopt a face-down position with the back of your head just breaking the surface

Using a 'duck dive' method of descending allows you to conserve more energy

lungs, allowing atmospheric pressure to push fresh air into your lungs through either your nose or mouth. Immersed in water, these muscular actions have to contend with the pressure of the water around your body. This is not a problem very close to the surface. Humans, however, having evolved to work at normal atmospheric pressures, the water pressure at even shallow depths is just too much to allow you to inhale. Breathing when your chest is submerged more than a third of a metre is very difficult and, if going deeper, breathing surface-pressure air through a snorkel becomes impossible.

So, underwater swimming with a snorkel means holding your breath and, of course, this limits the length of your dive. Taking a deeper breath will allow you to extend that time, but not by much. A better way to increase your underwater duration is to improve the efficiency of your submersion and swimming techniques. The slower you burn energy, the longer your air will last. Submerging with the minimum of effort and finning efficiently when submerged will prolong your snorkel dives and will also make you a better scuba diver. Taking a lung full of air will increase your buoyancy and this means you will have

to swim downwards in order to stay underwater. In order to leave the surface it is possible, if you are already finning forwards, to take a breath, angle the body down and then propel yourself under the surface by finning downwards. This is very difficult to do without a lot of splashing of fins on the surface, and consequent waste of effort. A better technique is to use a 'duck dive'. From a stationary position at the surface, take a breath then pivot to make a right-angle at the hips so your head is aimed straight down. Swing your legs up vertically out of the water so that their weight provides an impetus to drive you downwards. Once your fins are submerged you start the long, slow fin strokes that are the mark of a good snorkel diver.

An alternative way of submerging is to position your body head-up vertically, hands by your sides, in the water. Fin strongly upwards while taking a breath, then stop finning and allow your weight to drive you back down and below the surface. Once submerged, simply bend yourself downwards and commence underwater finning. With practice both of these methods can be performed very efficiently with the minimum of splashing and so are less likely to frighten the underwater creatures you are diving to observe.

More diving skills **111**

A snorkeller at the surface

The duck dive has the advantage of allowing you to continue to observe what is happening underwater throughout the submersion process. Always make sure there is a sufficient depth of water below you to perform these manoeuvres – piling into the bottom is neither good for you, nor the environment.

While swimming underwater, your body processes are consuming the oxygen content of the breath you took and at some stage it will all be consumed. When the oxygen levels fall low, your body will progressively start to shut down. At an early stage you will become unconscious, in a manner similar to fainting. Underwater this is obviously very dangerous and likely to quickly lead to death by drowning. Interestingly, your desire to breathe is triggered not by a lack of oxygen, but by the build-up of the carbon dioxide that is produced by your metabolic process. This trigger level is normally reached well before the oxygen content of your breath is all consumed. As long as you heed this need-to-breathe signal by returning to the surface to breathe, you can enjoy a long and happy snorkelling life. However, there is one big 'no-no' associated with snorkel diving. Before taking that breath which is going to last the length of your underwater excursion, it is very tempting to take

a number of deep practice breaths, a process termed 'hyperventilation'. This can be very dangerous, as it has the effect of flushing out your lungs and so lowering your carbon dioxide levels to leave them unnaturally low. In turn, this means that when you make your dive it is possible for your body to reach oxygen levels low enough to cause unconsciousness before carbon dioxide levels stimulate need-to-breathe signals. So do not hyperventilate when diving!

Once underwater, snorkellers are affected by the same pressure changes as scuba divers. As you descend, you will need to balance the increasing external pressure of the water on your eardrum. As the air in your lungs will automatically be subjected to the external water pressure, it will be at a similar pressure to the water pressing on your eardrum. Hence, following the same 'ear clearing' process of swallowing or nose pinching and pressurising will allow balancing of the pressures. Also, do not forget to breathe out a little air from your nose into your dive mask to prevent mask squeeze.

While you are underwater, the air in your snorkel tube will bubble out. Don't worry, you won't fill up with water. Because you are holding your breath, it will not even enter your mouth – unless you consciously

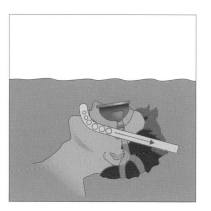

Begin to exhale before you reach the surface

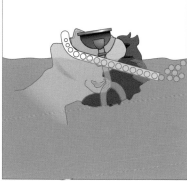

By the time you break the surface the water will have been expelled

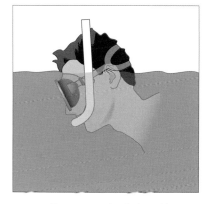

You can now begin breathing as normal

suck in the water. However, when you get to the surface you will need to get rid of this water. Simply copy the whale, by using the air in your lungs to make an explosive exhalation, creating an impressive water spout and so clearing your snorkel for breathing. It is always wise when breathing through a snorkel to breathe in gently, just in case a few water drops are left in it or a passing wave takes the opportunity to splash some water in. A useful technique is to curl your tongue to prevent such water droplets hitting the back of your throat, to guard against the coughing and spluttering such occasions can cause.

Probably the greatest risk posed to snorkel divers is the risk of being run down by other water users in surface craft. Submerged, you are invisible to them, and even at the surface you are very difficult to spot. You should listen and look for dangers as you surface, but the speed of modern leisure power craft and the silence of sailing craft can make this difficult.

A better solution is to place a distinctive buoy on the surface, which marks your diving zone, together with a buddy who remains at the surface while you dive. Your buddy can actively warn off surface craft and, if a fellow snorkeller, can take turns with you to dive. Use a 'one up, one down' procedure.

Following these few sensible rules gives safe and enjoyable access to some of our most colourful and interesting waters. Snorkelling can be the key to learning to swim for all ages, because it instils water confidence. As snorkelling skills are directly transferable, snorkelling is often the catalyst that leads people to learn to scuba dive. Surprisingly, at its most basic level, tourist scuba diving is probably simpler to perform, as breathing from a snorkel requires more skill than breathing from a regulator. If you start with scuba, transferring your skills to snorkelling should not be too difficult, while moving from snorkelling to scuba should prove a very simple step, as many snorkel-trained children have proved.

A diver breathes from his buddy's alternate air source (AAS)

Problem solving – alternate air source

It is a small step from removing and replacing your primary regulator underwater to learning how to breathe from an AAS. This will allow you to cope, in the unlikely event that the second stage of your own regulator fails. Should you decide to progress to more advanced diving techniques at a later stage, you may well have back-up breathing gas supplies delivered through a second regulator from a second diving cylinder. In this case, too, the ability to competently swap regulators underwater is essential. The procedure is simply to remove the AAS mouthpiece from its stowage point, or otherwise locate it, place it in your mouth, either purging it or blowing it clear of water

and begin breathing from it. Such a situation calls for immediate termination of the dive, and the need to ascend should be communicated to your buddy or dive leader and the rest of the dive aborted. Take care that the abandoned primary second stage does not catch on any obstruction, particularly any ascent or decompression lines you may encounter.

Should you, through bad planning, bad dive control or some other unfortunate circumstance, find you have consumed all your air during a dive, you will need a different alternate source of air. The nearest should be the AAS of your buddy and using this is only slightly more complex than using your own. The keys to success with this technique are positioning and contact. You need to be positioned so that the AAS regulator is correctly, comfortably and securely fitted in your mouth, and ideally so that you have eye contact with each other. As you are now using a breathing source fitted to your buddy's equipment, there must be a secure form of contact between the pair of you. Fortunately, diving equipment normally provides a number of secure hand-grip possibilities and you will be taught to use one which is appropriate to the equipment you are using. As such an event must signal the termination of the dive, that contact must not interfere with the necessarily close ascent you will both then have to make. It should also leave each of you with one hand free, which you will need to control buoyancy during the ascent. Remember that as buddies you each act as safety diver for the other. You need to master this skill in order to be proficient in both roles: that of receiving air from a buddy's AAS and providing your buddy with air from your own AAS.

Self-rescue

It has long been understood that people who live near water should know how to swim and, ideally, should have at least some basic skills in rescue and resuscitation. As people who deliberately enter the water to pursue our activity, this must also apply to divers, and to an even higher degree. The best principle is always to avoid trouble and hopefully your training will provide you with the knowledge and skills to apply prevention rather than cure. But it is also wise to be prepared for problems, because this forethought could be just the thing to allow you to catch the problem at an early stage when it is easier to prevent or solve. To this end, thinking through various scenarios in advance and working out self-rescue solutions can provide you with the tools to resolve difficult situations. Hopefully your buddy will be able to play a role in these solutions, but in some circumstances a self-contained answer may be preferable or even inevitable. Use of your own AAS is of course an example of self-rescue and an extreme, though rare, solution would involve making an emergency ascent to the surface without assistance from your buddy.

While the most likely cause would be lack of breathing air, even this situation has a number of variations, depending on the cause and associated

In a self rescue, it may be necessary to remove your weight belt

circumstances. Failure to check air consumption may cause you to inadvertently run out of air while you are a long distance from your buddy. The cure is simple – better diving practice.

Safe return to the surface is a key factor of the rescue, and so buoyancy and buoyancy control are going to be crucial. Changes to buoyancy can be made in two ways, either by removing sources of negative buoyancy or by the creation of positive buoyancy. Introducing further air into a BC or drysuit will create more positive buoyancy and, if sufficient, will precipitate an ascent. Finning upwards will also assist with ascent. Most fully equipped divers also have to carry a weight belt in order to achieve neutral buoyancy. It therefore follows that jettisoning this weight belt will also contribute towards achieving positive buoyancy. Most diver-training agencies recommend ditching the weight belt in such emergencies and include this procedure in their training programmes. Maybe because it is an irreversible action or maybe through a natural reluctance to abandon equipment, weight-belt ditching rarely seems to occur in anger.

For your personal safety, it is good practice to plan and train for this eventuality, ensuring that

Buddy rescue

A diver empties air from his buddy's BC to allow for a controlled ascent

you can always reach and operate your weight belt quick-release and then jettison it so it will fall clear without snagging other equipment. If the prime cause of this self-rescue is a lack of breathing air, it could well mean that there is a corresponding lack of buoyancy inflation air, making ditching the weight belt or finning the only options. When a dive cylinder is breathed down to 'empty', it is of course not completely empty of air. You cannot 'suck' all the air out of such a rigid container. When you reduce the air pressure in the cylinder to bring it close to that of the surrounding water, the regulator no longer has a pressure differential with which to operate, so no more air is delivered. Should this occur at a depth of say 20m, then by ascending to 10m you would again create a small pressure differential (1 bar). This means that during the ascent, as the ambient pressure reduces, you may be able to extract a little more air from the cylinder, either for breathing or buoyancy.

Whether positive buoyancy is achieved by ditching your weight belt or by inflating your BC or drysuit, it is important to try to keep control of your ascent rate. The greatest danger is from the air expanding in your lungs, so you should exhale continuously while ascending. Your lungs are not equipped with

overpressure sensors, so this needs to be a conscious action on your part. Naval personnel practising submarine escape ascents are trained to make a 'kissing' shape with open lips and blow steadily to exhaust the expanding air in their lungs. A similar exhalation, while retaining the mouthpiece in place, would seem the best advice to divers making a comparable rapid ascent. Once the surface is reached the first priority is to make sure you stay there. If it has not already been abandoned, this may be a good moment to get rid of any weight belt. BC inflation may be possible from your scuba set – if not, use mouth inflation to ensure you have plenty of positive buoyancy. Once this has been accomplished, use all means possible – visual and sound signals – to attract the assistance of your surface support party.

Buddy rescue

Much of the above advice applies to buddy rescue. Here we have to consider two main situations, the rescue of a conscious or unconscious buddy. Most rescues of a conscious buddy would result from air supply shortages and therefore follow the AAS procedure described earlier. Remember to take great care over positioning, maintaining secure contact and control of ascent rate through buoyancy. In your consideration of this scenario, think it through and practise it by playing both roles, casualty and rescuer.

More serious is the rescue of an unconscious diver. In this situation speed is obviously a priority with the twin aim of both you and your buddy arriving safely at the surface. A casualty who is unconscious underwater is going to remain there and inevitably become a fatality unless removed from the water, so that must be the first priority. To help ensure this will be the case, it is primarily the casualty's buoyancy that needs to become positive, so adjusting that from the outset is the most logical step to take. Positive casualty buoyancy can be created by either controlled BC inflation or by weight-belt ditching. If there is inflation air available, this would be the preferred method, as you are then already in control of the main buoyancy adjustment system. No big change of grip will be needed to vent excess buoyancy in order to keep ascent speed within reasonable bounds. While this buoyancy control occupies one of your hands, your other hand will need to be used to keep a positive grip on the casualty. You may also need it to vent your own

A buddy signals the surface team for assistance

BC, both when commencing the rescue and as you approach the surface. If the casualty's mouthpiece has been dislodged there may be some merit in reinserting it, but this should not be allowed to interfere with the main objectives of secure contact and as rapid an ascent as is prudent. Once the surface is reached ensure that the casualty cannot sink – it is possible that you will need to orally inflate their BC – and then use all means to attract urgent assistance from your surface support party. At this stage you will need to assess whether or not you need to start towing the casualty towards further assistance on the shore or in the cover boat. Full consideration of such an unfortunate eventuality should encourage you to regularly check the cylinder air pressures of both yourself and your buddy and may also persuade you to obtain a specialist diver rescue qualification. ☐

Chapter seven
A different world

Living in gaseous surroundings and glued by gravity to a fairly solid platform, we are accustomed to the way things happen in such an environment. Our sensory system is tuned to this setting, to the way light is perceived and sounds are heard and to the way we and objects around us are affected by the force of gravity. One of the major attractions of scuba diving is the exposure to totally new sensations. Light, sound and gravity all provide very different experiences to those we know above the surface. Understanding some of the reasons for these diversities increases your understanding and enjoyment of the world below the waves.

A different world
Light

Near the surface there is less loss of colour

One of the major attractions of diving is the amazing variety of life forms underwater and the vast range of colours in which they come. What is strange is that it is only in relatively shallow waters we can see the full range of colour of these exotic plants and animals. Above the surface we are accustomed to the objects we view being illuminated by natural light or sunlight.

The colour we perceive an object to be is the result of the light of that colour being reflected into our eyes. We notice that colours seen under artificial light look somewhat different, subtly or dramatically altered by the nature of the light source, such as in the home, shop or nightclub.

Underwater, the natural light has to pass through more and more water as depth increases. As the light passes through this water, different colours are gradually and progressively absorbed. If a colour is not present in the light source, an object of that colour will appear dark. Indeed, if the object is purely that colour it will appear black. Natural sunlight consists of a wide spectrum of colours that we observe distinctly from time to time as a rainbow. Underwater, these colours fade away with increasing depth – starting with the loss of colour from the red end of the colour spectrum. This means that even at a depth of 10m, any objects coloured red appear dark, and by the time we are at 30m we are in a very blue-grey world.

What is amazing is that if we illuminate this deeper

Seeing underwater without a mask

Seeing underwater with a mask

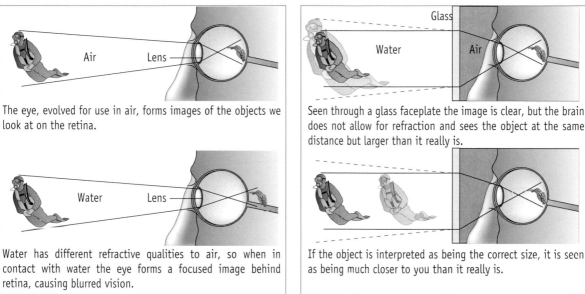

The eye, evolved for use in air, forms images of the objects we look at on the retina.

Seen through a glass faceplate the image is clear, but the brain does not allow for refraction and sees the object at the same distance but larger than it really is.

Water has different refractive qualities to air, so when in contact with water the eye forms a focused image behind retina, causing blurred vision.

If the object is interpreted as being the correct size, it is seen as being much closer to you than it really is.

Your vision underwater is affected by water and – because of your dive mask – a change in refraction. It is interesting to note that the image on the retina is always inverted, so your brain 'sees' the world upside down and automatically adjusts to provide you with a right-way-up perception of your surroundings.

world using artificial light, such as that from a torch, we often find that the plants and animals living here have as wide a range of colouring as those near the surface. For this very reason many divers include a waterproof torch in their kit for all dives, not only for those undertaken at night.

In addition to absorbing colours, water has another major effect on the way light travels through it. This affects us whenever the light enters or leaves water at any angle other than perpendicular (90°). Whenever this transition occurs the angle of the light ray is slightly altered – the technical term is 'refracted'. It is most obvious if we simply submerge and open our eyes. No matter how clear the water, everything appears blurred. This is because the light reflected from an object no longer enters our eyes at an angle we can properly bring to focus on the retina. Our eyes have evolved to function properly in air, so wearing a diving face mask solves a major part of this problem. It does not completely solve it, because a certain amount of refraction occurs as the light passes from water to glass and then to air. With normal eyesight, focusing is not a problem, but the refraction causes us to underestimate our distance from the object. Reach for something underwater and you will find your arm appears to be shorter! Another way our brain interprets this phenomenon is to believe an object is larger than it really is – hence divers' tales of enormous lobsters!

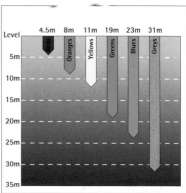

The loss of colour as we go deeper starts with red and continues through orange, yellow, green, blue and grey

Although often described as 'the silent world', you will hear lots of things underwater

Sound

Travelling through water also affects the behaviour of sound waves and thus our sense of hearing. Essentially, sound travels much faster through the denser medium of water, approximately 25 times as fast as through air. When our brain interprets the sounds we hear normally, it calculates the direction from where the sounds come. This calculation is based on the speed at which the sound travels and the precise timing of the sound signalled by each of our ears. With the sound travelling so much faster underwater, this highly accurate time measurement is upset and our ability to assign a direction to the sound is greatly reduced. This means sound signalling by your dive buddy or noise from a boat engine can be heard, but it is difficult to allocate a direction to the sound.

As has been said, sound waves travel so much faster because the water is much denser than air. However, this same density means the energy of the sound waves in our normal hearing range is more quickly absorbed, so the range of sounds is smaller. To some, this means underwater can be described as 'the silent world'. Once you are accustomed to it you will find it is far from silent.

The sound of your own bubbles and those of your buddy can be clearly heard. So too the sound of passing boats with high-pitched outboard engines, or big ships with rumbling diesel engines. While fish are not too talkative, the snapping noises of various crustaceans and molluscs can often be clearly heard.

While on the subject of sound, our normal vocal communication system is not very effective underwater. Firstly, it is very difficult to articulate speech with a regulator in your mouth. Even if you remove your regulator, speaking into the water does not produce the same effect as speaking into air. The sounds are very distorted and tend to be further obscured by the noise of the bubbles you produce in trying to speak.

Even then the effects of pressure have another trick to play on us. As we go deeper and breathe air under greater pressure, the density of our breathing gas becomes greater. As our vocal chords are used to operating with one atmosphere air, the sounds they produce become higher pitched. Gradually, as depth increases, this effect also degrades our speech-making ability until we are making noises more appropriate to Donald Duck.

The sounds of marine animals can sometimes be heard by divers

Buoyancy

Being neutrally buoyant feels as though you are free from gravity

Gravity

One of the most enjoyable aspects of being in the water is the apparent escape from gravity. Of course, we are not free of gravity, but the overall density of a human being is very close to that of water. This means that if we are naked and fully immersed in water, depending on the amount of air in our lungs, we will either float or just sink. Most people when relaxed will float with their lungs filled at normal capacity. Unfortunately, our natural floating position is face-down, with the top and back of the head just awash. As we breathe through the front of our head, this relaxed position does not assist in normal breathing. This is where the simple addition of a snorkel to transfer our breathing point to somewhere near the back of our head is a real life-saver. A few people think that they are negatively buoyant, but in the vast majority of cases this is because they experience difficulty in keeping a very heavy part of their body, the head, above the surface. Even with the lungs fully inflated this is often difficult as it requires considerable positive buoyancy.

Wearing heavy clothing or equipment will, of course, tend to make us sink more rapidly.

Although diving equipment is heavy out of the water, once immersed the overall effect of all the equipment on us is to make us float, so a weight belt has to be worn in order to dive comfortably. Ideally, the combination of protective clothing, scuba and other equipment will be made neutral by the addition of the weight belt. The BC can then be used for fine trimming, adjusting for things such as the increased weight of air in the cylinder at the start of the dive, or the loss of wetsuit buoyancy which comes with increased pressure.

A further consideration is the distribution of weight and buoyancy around the diver. Typically, buoyancy tends to be grouped around the upper body and the weights low around the waist, making the diver adopt a head-up position. While this is fine at the surface, a horizontal attitude is usually a more comfortable position when diving. This is another reason to achieve neutral buoyancy with as little weight as possible. If it is very difficult to arrive at a comfortable underwater attitude, check the problem is not caused by bad positioning of the cylinder. Conversely, if you find you have too much buoyancy in the legs, possibly from air migration in a drysuit, consider wearing ankle weights.

The water itself – salt and fresh

While most divers prefer diving in the seas and oceans of our planet, there is much to be seen in fresh water too. A lot of diving takes place at inland freshwater sites such as lakes and flooded quarries, mainly for reasons of access. These can provide ideal sheltered-water conditions for diver training and are frequently less affected by adverse weather than more exposed coastal waters. Freshwater sites can also have a charm of their own, whether it be the different underwater plant and animal life or the often dramatic topography of underwater cliffs and rock formations.

Like the sea, freshwater visibility is usually affected by the recent weather. Recent rains can cause feeder streams and rivers to discharge great volumes of silt-laden water, thus creating poor visibility conditions until the silt settles. This same silt can then be disturbed by carelessly finning divers, recreating that same poor visibility. River outlet areas of the sea are most susceptible to this effect, but these muddy waters are also moved by tidal streams, so coastal waters may see visibility changes with varying states of the tide.

Some inland waters, especially in cave and cavern systems, can have absolutely stunning clarity of water making them an underwater photographer's dream. Beware, though, cave diving is a speciality of its own and requires very particular training usually with specific cave diving equipment. Generally speaking, it is considered easier to train a caver to dive than a diver to cave.

Water is at its densest at a temperature of around 4°C, which means water at this temperature will sink to the bottom, while – normally – the warmer, less dense water will be at the surface. If water becomes cooler than 4°C, its density decreases and it will rise to the surface where with further cooling it will become even less dense and float as ice. Diving under ice also requires special training and techniques, and should not be undertaken lightly.

Usually there will be a gradual reduction in water temperature as a diver descends, but sometimes a body of warmer water will move independently from the colder water beneath. This can then give rise to sudden temperature changes when moving between these two bodies of water. The boundary is referred to as a 'thermocline' and can often be seen as an oily-looking shimmering layer in the water.

Inland dive sites are often used for training purposes

Wave action at the surface can have
an effect on entry to and exit from
a dive site

The way the water moves

Most inland dive sites are relatively small and the waters in them fairly static. Obvious exceptions are rivers, which can be interesting dive sites if proper respect is given to the possible currents. A fully equipped diver will find it hard work to swim at even 0.5 knots (0.9km per hour) so quite small currents can cause problems for divers. This also applies to sea diving, where tidal flows can easily exceed the diver's swimming capability. Provided suitable precautions are taken regarding surface cover and exit facilities, diving with the flow of the current (drift diving) can be interesting and exhilarating – again, remember that this is a skill requiring appropriate training.

Tidal currents are caused by interactions between the gravitational forces of the Sun, Moon and Earth, coupled with the rotation of the earth. As the Earth rotates, most sea areas experience two high tides and two low tides each day. As the interval between high and low water is about 6 hours 15 minutes, the actual time changes each day.

Current is generally strongest halfway between high and low water, but there can be significant variations caused by the impact of coastal or sea bed topography. Additionally, there is an overlying 28-day lunar cycle, with alternating maximum or spring tides and minimum or neap tides occurring some seven days apart. Some sea areas such as the Mediterranean have very small tidal variations which can be cancelled out by wind or even temperature-driven water movements.

The principal cause of surface movement is the wind

The interaction of two worlds

Other types of water movement can also have a considerable effect on our diving activities. The vertical movement of the surface can greatly affect how we enter the water from the shore, our travel, pre-dive and post-dive boating activities and the dive itself. The principal cause of surface movement is the wind, but beware – a particular sea state may have been caused by a wind a considerable distance away and even some days before. Once underwater, the action of the waves at the surface diminishes as depth increases, though big storms can have a significant effect even as deep as 30m. Our main concerns are wave action affecting entry and exit, surface swimming or when diving in fairly shallow water near rocks or a shipwreck. Kitting up and moving to the exit point on a rolling boat is not easy, nor is passing up heavy equipment and climbing a ladder in such conditions. This means it is important that those organising dives have some understanding of weather forecasting and weather influence over the sites that they are planning to dive. □

Chapter eight
What next?

Diving is a very new human activity and you should by now realise that the knowledge and skills covered so far are just the basics of what will be an ongoing education. As a diver you have the chance to be a genuine explorer of truly unknown regions of our planet, yet, need only a relatively modest support infrastructure which is easily available. So, what are you going to do now that the door to our underwater world is opened to you?

What next?
Marine life

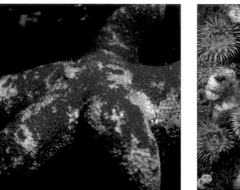

Bloody Henry starfish

Daisy anemones

Tubeworms

Great pleasure can be had simply by diving under the waves and looking around. You can observe the amazing variety of life forms and their environmental adaptation or study the multiplicity of plant and animal life, which varies in scale from microscopic plants to the world's largest mammals. All levels of interest can be satisfied – you can simply look, you can 'train spot', ticking off the creatures you observe and recognise from brightly coloured underwater guide slates. Or, by studying marine biology, you can let this interest lead you down a never-ending path. Courses are available at all levels, from those for absolute beginners to specialists focusing on specific branches of marine life. A large portion of the new knowledge of the undersea environment has come, and is still coming, from new and enthusiastic 'amateur' biologists. Groups of 'ordinary' divers acting as a team can work as the eyes of marine scientists, visiting particular sites at various intervals and conducting environmental observations and surveys. Now that you have taken the important first steps and entered the underwater world, why not learn some more about that world? Marine life identification courses are available to divers of all levels and can make an excellent entry point leading to more specialised and advanced studies in marine biology. Whatever your level of interest, always remember that your goal should be to protect and preserve the underwater habitat and its occupants, interfering with the delicate balance of nature as little as possible.

Common octopus

Nudibranch

Compass jellyfish

Sponge

Devonshire cup coral

Gorgonian fan coral

Marine worm

Blue-spotted ray

Blue shark

Underwater photography is comprised of four elements: the visibility, the equipment, the technical competence of the photographer and the artistic capability of the photographer

Some underwater cameras are completely waterproof and do not require separate housings

Underwater photographs serve as an ocean-friendly reminder of your dives

Photography

As a diver, you will want to communicate your observations and experiences to others, especially those who have yet to follow in your fin strokes. Taking pictures and shooting film or video are obvious ways of sharing what you have seen. A word of warning: if your ordinary photograph album is full of shots of your thumb, relatives with missing heads and fuzzy landscapes, your underwater pictures are likely to have similar results. There are four main ingredients in recording underwater images – the visibility, the equipment, the technical competence of the photographer and the artistic capability of the photographer. The first is largely a matter of what kind of underwater experiences you wish to record. If it involves diving around coral reefs, finding good visibility is not too difficult, but if it is in the North Atlantic, obtaining the best visibility can be time consuming and mastering successful photography in difficult conditions requires even more experimentation and patience. The equipment you select is going to be affected by your available budget, but quality and choice are constantly improving and as the market expands so costs are falling.

Those of you with a practical bent may follow in the footsteps of the first underwater photographers by adapting and constructing your own waterproof housings and other equipment.

The third ingredient, technical competence, is not too difficult to acquire – there are many specialist books available as well as training courses run by experts. Depending on your existing ability, even books and training covering dry-land photography might be an advisable first step. Early underwater photographers used land equipment secured in waterproof housings with transparent windows. Problems of sealing mechanisms used to operate the controls and of pressurising the housing had to be solved, together with those of providing and synchronising additional lighting. Today, there is a choice of professional housings for a number of cameras – still, movie and video – together with a range of waterproof flash and movie lighting units. There are even a number of cameras that are waterproof in themselves, requiring no additional housing and so making operation of the various controls much simpler.

Photography

Housings allow land cameras to be used underwater

Shipwrecks make good photographic subjects

Special wide-angle and macro lenses, adapted for underwater use, are available and films can be specially processed to account for the colour balances encountered underwater.

Extra lighting can be particularly difficult in less than perfect visibility. Any suspended matter between the camera lens and the object you are trying to capture will block light from the object, much like trying to see through a mist. Even worse, if you try to illuminate the object from a light source close to the lens, not only will the suspended matter reduce light reaching the object, it will reflect light back into the lens. This is rather like trying to see through fog with the main beams of a car's headlights – the reflected light blinds, and obscures what you are trying to see. Matters are improved if the light source is removed as far as practicable from the camera and is used in order to illuminate the scene from an angle. You should bear this problem in mind when considering cameras with built-in flashes, as they are only really suitable for use in very good visibility or at very short range.

Artistic success is difficult to achieve, but bear in mind that it is extremely rare to find a successful artist who has not undergone some form of training, formal or otherwise. If you can look at the work of other photographers and decide what it is that pleases or displeases you, you have already made some artistic judgements and can use these as a base to guide your own work. Your abilities can be further developed by reading books, attending courses and discussing your pictures with other photographers and divers. You will find that even the most successful photographers have many more failures than successes and rightly regard film as the least expensive part of any photo shoot. In shooting film and video professionally, with a well-scripted story and an organised set, a 7 to 1 rejection ratio is regarded as quite normal. Most artists become their own most severe critics, so do not despair if instant success is not yours – perseverance is required. One aspect of underwater photography is the need for an understanding dive buddy who is sympathetic to a photographer's needs.

There is a danger that the photographer can become rather single-minded on the photographic task and an understanding buddy will compensate for this. This same buddy, besides often serving as photographic model, may also serve as an artistic critic.

As a rule of thumb, the most difficult images to

Underwater video systems are increasingly sophisticated and offer high performance

produce successfully are black and white ones. Here, the critical viewer has no distraction of colour or movement and it is the technical and artistic qualities of the image that bear the full brunt of conveying your message. With colour pictures, the observer has an extra visual channel and the tones, shades and composition of the colours can compensate for other possible weaknesses in the work. Once movement is added, the viewer is even more distracted from absolute measurements of the image, as can well be observed by freeze-framing a video. Quality that would be regarded as unacceptable in a still picture is rendered quite presentable in a movie format. It must also be remembered that the best pictures are

those that tell a story or at least make an interesting statement. Photographic still shots, of course, tell short stories, but for films to be really successful there must be an identifiable story linking the sequences together. Time spent in developing a storyboard and planning film sequences and camera angles will always be time well spent. Do not forget the limitations placed on underwater filming by mundane factors such as air consumption, decompression requirements, thermal tolerances or even tide times.

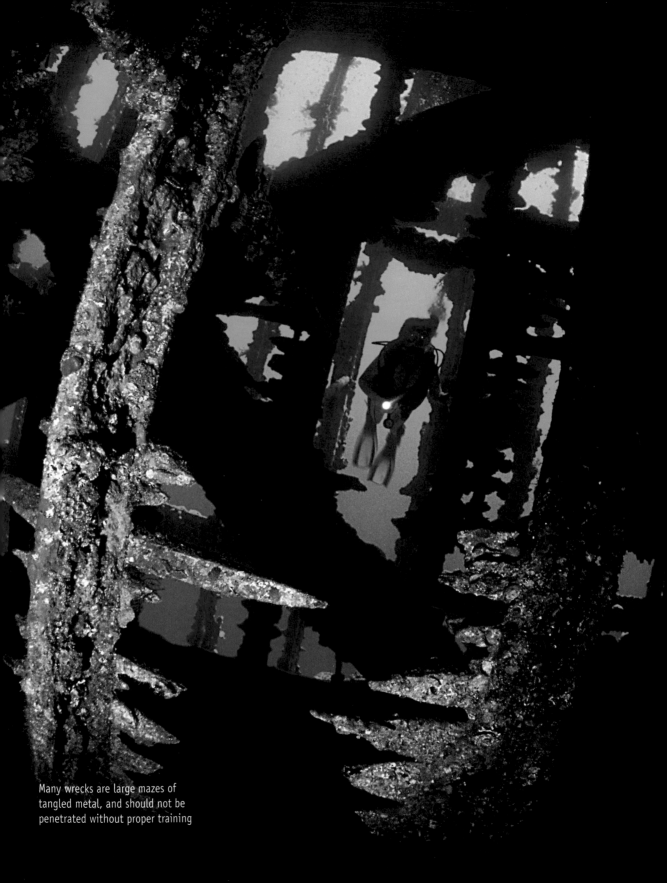

Many wrecks are large mazes of
tangled metal, and should not be
penetrated without proper training

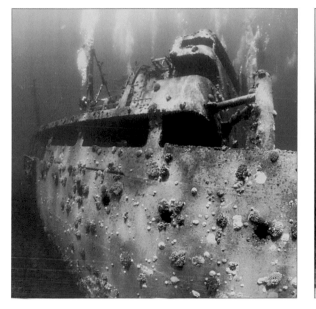

Corals and other marine creatures slowly colonise wrecks

Shipwrecks make for atmospheric dives

Diving into history

Many scuba divers find diving submerged wrecks a fascinating activity. A flooded ship can provide an ideal habitat for a great many forms of aquatic life, making it an absorbing dive for fish-watchers and even the most serious marine biologist. This same underwater life, coupled with the often atmospheric environments created by the ship itself, can also make such sites a paradise for photographers. Some divers are irresistibly drawn to diving shipwrecks. These are divers who find great satisfaction in locating lost wrecks, in positively identifying them, in studying their condition and researching their history. Some wrecks demand exploration, others evoke feelings of awe and respect because of the drama of their sinking, or the loss of life involved.

Diving shipwrecks can be very different to the dives you undertake during your initial diver training. Most wrecks in shallow waters tend to be quickly broken up and dispersed by the enormous power of surface waves. When diving such sites it can be difficult to comprehend how the broken and twisted masses of metal, usually encrusted with rust, weed and molluscs, ever went together to form a ship. Wooden

parts disappear fairly quickly, followed by the steel plates as rust takes its toll in the highly oxygenated surface waters. More durable are the thicker metallic masses such as engines, condensers and boilers, steel girders and frames, propellers and propeller shafts and the many parts made from brass or bronze.

These tangled mazes can create confusing navigational problems, the more so as your dive compass is often made useless by the surrounding iron and steel. If visibility is poor, sometimes these location problems can be solved by reeling out a distance line to help find the way back to the descent/ascent line or shot-line. But these are techniques awaiting you in more advanced training, together with techniques for exploring the more intact wrecks that are usually found in deeper waters.

Not all wrecks are of shipping. Aircraft, amphibious military vehicles, even railway trains and road vehicles have all found their way to the bottom of the sea. Mankind, throughout its history has used water as a medium for transport, but has also lived over the water. In many parts of the world, houses and settlements have been constructed on pilings rising

Archaeology

Underwater archaeology is an exacting task, which requires the diver to take accurate records

Responsible divers will consider themselves guardians of underwater treasures

above the water's surface. Long since destroyed and lost to land-bound exploration, these sites now provide archaeologically trained divers with numerous opportunities to study the ways in which some of our ancestors lived. While most of this research involves archaeologists who have become divers, much is also conducted by divers who, having made underwater discoveries, have been sufficiently motivated to obtain the necessary archaeological training. One of the most famous shipwrecks of British naval history, King Henry VIII's battleship the Mary Rose, was successfully charted, archaeologically excavated and prepared for recovery to its Portsmouth museum by a small team of professional diving archaeologists who worked for several years guiding hundreds of amateur divers.

Recreational diving is rather young to have developed traditions and fortunately has shown fairly rapid evolution, not only in equipment, but also in customs. Many of the first divers used their new-found underwater abilities to hunt the sea life they found, and not always too discriminately. Those same divers are now ardent conservationists, having

witnessed the damage such activities could wreak. Similarly, early wreck divers sought souvenirs of the wrecks they visited. This has been replaced by an understanding of our responsibility as guardians of these underwater treasures. Every wreck is a story, a page from history, and many of these chronicles have yet to be unravelled and properly understood. Careless intervention can make this task difficult or impossible and shipwrecks are not a renewable resource. Fortunately, the brass-happy pirate image whose success was measured by the weight of scrap metal recovered has been replaced by a serious and responsible attitude to the protection of our underwater heritage. Photographs replace souvenirs taken from the oceans, and if you really do want to show your friends, children, partners or parents these underwater treasures, well, take them diving with you. Diver training is open to all.

Opportunities for underwater historical research are not limited to sites of watery catastrophes. Today's massive pollution of the oceans by our industrial and commercial irresponsibility has a long history; it is only the scale and potential for damage

Measurements and illustrations need to be made when relics are brought to the surface

Underwater hockey or 'octopush' is now an international sport

that has changed. As long as mankind has used water for travel, items (rubbish) have been lost or thrown overboard. Some of these items have proved very durable and have become interesting relics that also help to fill in the patchwork of history. While many discoveries of this type are accidental, there are places where these activities were concentrated, such as close to ancient moorings. Many of these sites are still busy with shipping today, so pay attention to the dangers posed by surface craft if you intend to dive these sites. Make sure you follow all local guidelines – there are usually rules and regulations governing activities in busy shipping lanes, harbours and designated sites. Abandoning or losing objects in the water also occurs from the shore. The waters around bridges and riverside pubs are classic examples, but ancient springs and wells have also been explored.

Underwater sport

On the whole, diving is a very non-competitive activity, but a desire to keep fit and improve basic skills in the early days of diving led to the development of the game of 'octopush'. This game consists of two opposing teams of players each equipped with mask, fins, snorkel and small, hand-carried 'pusher', trying to move a lead-weighted 'squid' or puck into the other's goal to score a 'gull'. This game, which is claimed to have originated within the Brighton branch of the British Sub-Aqua Club, is now played internationally, with national leagues, and is more commonly referred to as underwater hockey. According to the rules, body contact is not allowed, and maybe through misinterpretation or dissatisfaction with this rule, a separate sport of underwater rugby has also developed. Some countries also include fringe activities such as equipment-assisted swimming racing.

Technical diving demands more equipment
and further training

Becoming a diving instructor can be very rewarding

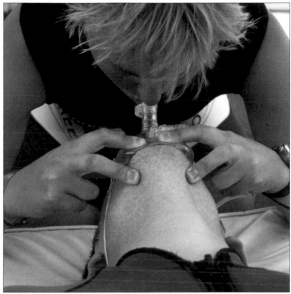
Training in first aid and rescue diving will improve your confidence

Personal development

Becoming a diver is for many a life-changing experience, a step in self-definition. It is not unusual, once those first underwater fin strokes have been made, for people's lives to be totally transformed. Many are drawn to sharing their own passion by teaching others, and this in itself can provide a new career. For others, the communications skills gained through instructing has given them advantages in their normal careers. Even the simple achievement of becoming a diver, and the self-confidence gained with it, has had a positive impact on the lives of many divers. However, that was not your prime motivation in taking the plunge. This book has been designed to help you through the early stages of diving. Your entry-level training should see you competent in the basic use of your equipment. It should provide you with enough knowledge and skill to enable you to safely dive as a member of a buddy pair, in waters and depths similar to those where your training took place. This is unlikely to be the limit of your underwater ambition and nor should it be: with some 70 per cent of our planet immersed in water there is always more for you to see that will be new and exciting.

Now you need to extend your diving capabilities and, surprise, surprise, the formula is very similar to that you have followed so far. Firstly, you can always improve and polish the skills you already have by increasing your diving experience. Performing more dives in the waters you are familiar with is a start. Broadening that experience by diving in similar conditions in other locations will help your development. Be aware that some adaptation may be necessary with changed conditions, especially where significant changes in visibility, water temperature or dive organisation are encountered. Seek assistance in coping with any such changes and, if needed, obtain formal training to provide the knowledge and experience you lack. If you wish to dive deeper, in a safe manner, you need further knowledge and skills. Always try to broaden your diving experience in progressive steps that are small enough to be easily and safely managed. For example, when changing to new equipment make sure you first master its use in controlled, non-challenging environments, before trying it in situations that also demand lots of attention for other tasks.

A continuing adventure

Boat handling is a useful skill for divers to learn

Diver-training agencies recognise that learning to dive is a progressive activity, involving a continuous increase in knowledge paralleled by an expansion of skills and experience. For convenience's sake, various stages in this process are evaluated and awarded titles or diver grades. Along with these grades is a summary of recommended limits of the depths and activities appropriate to that level of training, in some places these limits having the weight of law behind them. These guidelines are only there for your protection and if you find them in any way limiting, the solution is quite simple. Study, train and gain the necessary experience to move to the next grade and the expanded horizons so offered. A parallel system of progressive grading is also applied to diving instructors.

Besides progression in simple diving grades there is a wealth of specialist diving activities to be explored. Some are activity oriented, such as those mentioned earlier, including underwater science, photography and archaeology. Some concentrate on rescue capability, ranging from basic life-saving techniques, first aid and therapeutic oxygen administration, to rescue management. Knowledge and skill in dive marshalling, seamanship, surface navigation, chartwork and position-fixing are seen as valuable to divers managing their own dive trips. For those wanting to push at the technical frontiers courses are available on extended range diving, the use of breathing gas mixtures other than air, rebreather diving and other associated topics.

The door is open – now you can learn more about your underwater world, plan new places to visit and new things to do when you get there. It is often said that the day you stop having new experiences and learning from your diving is the day to stop diving. Hopefully, that is a situation you will never experience, your diving will be a continuing adventure! ■

Now that your initial training is complete, you can continue your underwater adventure
by learning new skills and using more advanced equipment

Appendix one – Decompression tables

Examples of BSAC decompression materials, available from the BSAC mailshop, website: www.bsac.org

Decompression tables

The BSAC is the only diver-training agency which uses decompression tables specifically designed for its members to use in recreational diving. These tables, researched by Dr Tom Hennessy and released in 1988, depart completely from the common usage of tables designed for military or commercial diving. Based on micro-bubble resolution rather than tissue simulation, Dr Hennessy's methodology has subsequently been adopted by astronauts engaged in the construction of the International Space Station. BSAC publishes the '88 Decompression Tables in three formats:

- A 'slide rule' dive calculator suitable for most sea level diving with reasonable surface intervals.
- A booklet containing four sets of the tables enabling diving to be conducted in a range of different atmospheric pressure bands, essential for altitude diving, together with complete instructions for use and worked examples.
- A booklet containing four sets of the tables enabling diving to be conducted with a range of different nitrox (nitrogen/oxygen) breathing gas mixtures, with a simple procedure for changing gas mixture on subsequent dives.

All three formats are printed on waterproof material and include instructions for use and a dive conduct slate to assist dive planning and control. A key feature of the BSAC '88 Decompression Tables is their simplicity of use, as they avoid the conventional need for residual nitrogen calculation. Another major difference is the use of 'dive time' (time to 6m), a procedure much more in tune with recreational diving, rather than the military/commercial style of 'bottom time' (time to leaving maximum depth). With the introduction of these tables, BSAC was a leader in variable ascent speeds, recommending a maximum ascent speed (rather than an obligatory target speed) to 6m and then a slower final ascent to the surface.

Using the BSAC '88 Decompression Tables

1 Select a Table to suit the surface air pressure and your tissue nitrogen saturation state (Current Tissue Code). For a first dive this is usually Table A (see example opposite).
2 Choose the maximum depth that you plan to reach during the dive – in this case 12m.
3 Move along that row to the right and select the time you expect to reach 6m on the final ascent to the surface, always choosing a greater time if you exact time is not shown. In this case the planned time is 30 minutes, so the 37-minute column is chosen.
4 Move vertically down that column to read your Surfacing Code, for this example it is C.
5 Note these figures on your dive conduct slate and repeat the procedure using the next time column and the next deeper depth row to create two fall-back solutions should you inadvertently exceed these dive parameters.
6 Follow your plan during the dive, observing maximum depth and time.
7 When you reach 6m during the final ascent, check that you have followed the plan and, if necessary, move to a fall-back plan.
8 Note your Surfacing Code and the time you exit the water.

BSAC '88 Tables require a maximum ascent speed of 15m per minute up to 6m and then you should take at least one minute to ascend the final 6m to the surface.

LEVEL 1 (greater than 984 milli…)
TABLE A

DEPTH (metres)	ASCENT (mins)	No-Stop Dives DIVE TIME
3	(1)	− 166 ∞
6	(1)	− 36 166 593 ∞
9	1	− 17 67 167 203 243 311 32
12	1	− 17 37 87 104 122 156 16
15	1	− 6 24 54 64 74 98 10
18	1	− 17 37 44 51 68 7
DECOMPRESSION STOPS (mins) at 6 metres		1
SURFACING CODE		B C D E F G
21	1	− 13 28 32 37 51 5
24	2	− 11 22 26 30 41 4
27	2	− 8 18 21 24 34 4
30	2	− 7 15 17 20 29 3

Note *there are some dives possible on Table **G** that produce a S… decompression stop.*

This SURFACE INTERVAL TABLE shows how your body tissues gradu… periods of time, whilst you remain at LEVEL 1. Enter the left hand colu… from your last dive and move right along that row for your SURFACE I… TISSUE CODE is indicated.

SURFACE INTERVAL TABLE L

Last Dive SURFACING CODE	15	30	Minutes 60	90	2	3	4
G	G	F	E	D		C	
F	F	E	D			C	
E	E		D		C		
D			D		C		
C	C		C				
B				B			
A						A	

Repeat diving

1 From the previous example use your Surfacing Code C and move across that row to the right until you are under your planned surface interval time.
2 Read the Current Tissue Code letter from that table cell to discover which Table to use for the next dive.
3 In the adjacent example Code C is retained until a surface interval of two hours has passed, when Table B can be used. Table A cannot be used until 12 hours has elapsed.

Safer diving

Because of the wide variations in human physiology and the large number of factors that can affect your susceptibility to decompression illness, no table can guarantee to protect you against all risk. Whenever diving please take the following into account.

1 The maximum recommended depth for sport diving using air is 50m and when carrying out two or more dives in one day perform the deepest dive first.
2 It is recommended that no more than three dives be performed in any 24-hour period and any dive series involving consecutive days diving to 30m-plus should be limited to four days, after which a 24-hour break should be taken.
3 It is advisable to limit any diving within a 24-hour period to dives requiring a total of 20 minutes of in-water stops.
4 Always be in control of your buoyancy, especially during the ascent, and observe the maximum recommended speeds 15m per minute to 6m and then one minute to the surface.
5 You can conduct slower descents and ascents, while remaining within the table limits for your dive but multiple 'saw-tooth' ascents and descents should be avoided.
6 Be aware that smoking, alcohol or drug consumption, tiredness, dehydration, age, increased body fat and any medical condition affecting the circulatory or respiratory systems are thought to increase your risk of decompression illness. So, too, can excessive physical exertion during or immediately after a dive.
7 Leave an appropriate Surface Interval before flying or ascending to altitude following diving - BSAC recommends at least 16 hours.

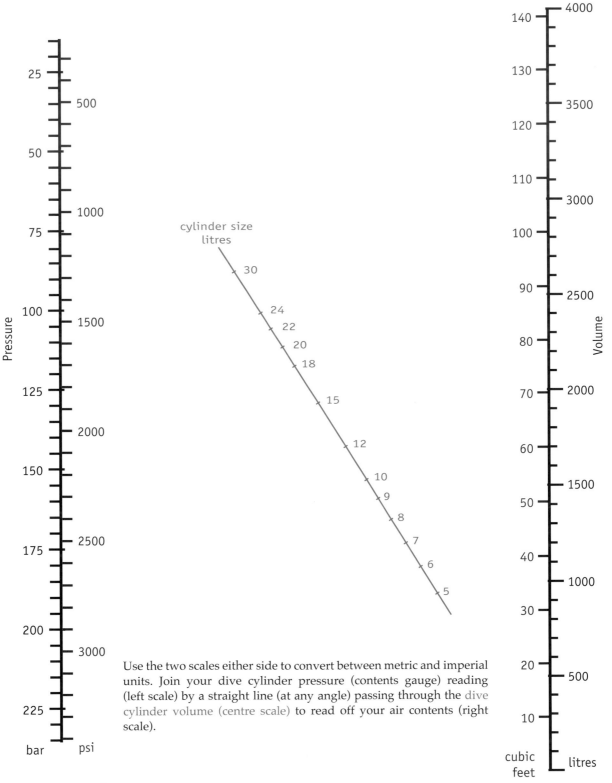

Use the two scales either side to convert between metric and imperial units. Join your dive cylinder pressure (contents gauge) reading (left scale) by a straight line (at any angle) passing through the dive cylinder volume (centre scale) to read off your air contents (right scale).

© 2002 Ellerby Dive Planner

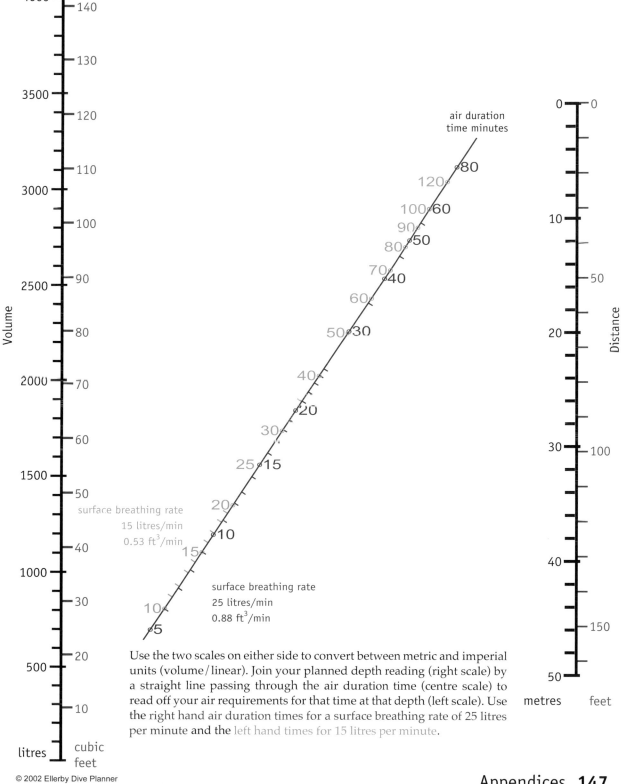

air duration
time minutes

Volume

litres

cubic
feet

surface breathing rate
15 litres/min
0.53 ft³/min

surface breathing rate
25 litres/min
0.88 ft³/min

Distance

metres

feet

Use the two scales on either side to convert between metric and imperial units (volume/linear). Join your planned depth reading (right scale) by a straight line passing through the air duration time (centre scale) to read off your air requirements for that time at that depth (left scale). Use the right hand air duration times for a surface breathing rate of 25 litres per minute and the left hand times for 15 litres per minute.

© 2002 Ellerby Dive Planner

Appendix three – First aid

The recovery position

The recovery position for an unstable environment such as a boat, note that one arm is arranged behind the body

First aid

The aim of administering first aid in any diving incident must be to preserve the life of the casualty – and all involved – with the minimum of intervention, in order to limit the effects of the incident and to promote recovery. Avoid compounding the situation by taking foolhardy risks to recover the casualty. With water-centred incidents, the correct actions in order of priority are:

- Reach for the casualty.
- Throw flotation aids.
- Wade out to the casualty or use surface transport or flotation to reach the casualty.
- Swim to the casualty. However, swimming alone should be considered a poorer, final option.

The sequence of action can be summarised as 'assessment, diagnosis and treatment'. Action priorities in order of importance are 'airway, breathing and circulation' (ABC), followed by incidents involving major bleeding and other conditions. Should there be more than one casualty, you should prioritise by treating the non-breathing casualty first, followed by the breathing but unconscious casualty and then any casualties suffering from major bleeding.

Drowning

In order to ensure a viable airway, the casualty's mouth and nose must be clear of the water, hence the need for divers to know how to lift non-breathing casualties to the surface. Ideally this should be followed by immediate removal of the casualty from the water. If this is not possible, stabilise the casualty at the surface and if he or she is still not breathing, commence artificial ventilation (AV). In-water AV can be administered either by mouth-to-nose or mouth-to-mouth resuscitation, with mouth-to-nose generally preferred. The ability of a single rescuer is fairly limited, so efforts should be made to summon assistance and to move to a situation where exit from the water is possible. A balance has to be struck between maintaining an effective rate of AV and moving the casualty towards a water exit.

AV on its own will not be enough if circulation has stopped. In these circumstances cardiac compression (CC) will be needed, requiring that the casualty is supported on a firm surface such as a boat or on land. To give effective cardio-pulmonary resuscitation (CPR) you should obtain appropriate training – courses are offered by most diver training agencies.

Barotrauma/DCI

The most serious pressure-related injuries (known as barotrauma) result from incorrect dive profiles as well as rapid ascents resulting in either decompression illness (DCI) or a burst lung or lungs. First-aid actions are the same for both.

Symptoms are
- Weakness, paralysis, numbness, tingling
- Vision problems, balance problems, confusion, convulsions, unconciousness
- Large-joint pain
- Skin itchiness or rash

Treatment
- Arrange immediate evacuation to recompression facilities
- Lay casualty flat, administer 100-per-cent oxygen
- If no other injuries or nausea, give isotonic fluids or water
- DO NOT attempt in-water treatment

Shock

In most accidents casualties will be suffering shock.
Symptoms are
- Weakness, faintness, giddiness, anxiousness, restlessness
- Nausea, vomiting, thirst, cold clammy skin, profuse sweating
- Shallow rapid breathing, rapid weak pulse

Treatment
- Treat prime cause, keep quiet, reassure, keep warm and comfortable
- Lay down with legs raised (not if DCI involved), administer 100-per-cent oxygen
- Monitor condition, evacuate to medical attention

External bleeding

Look for signs of visible blood loss.
Treatment
- Direct pressure or indirect pressure to pressure points

Internal bleeding

Symptoms are
- Signs of shock without obvious blood loss
- Pain out of all proportion to visible damage
- Pattern bruising, coughing/spitting blood, blood in urine/faeces

Treatment:
- Treat as for shock
- Urgent evacuation
- Check and record breathing and pulse and level of response every ten minutes
- Put in recovery position if unconscious

Fractures

Symptoms are:
- Sound at initial break, visible bone ends/deformity/loss of power
- Pain, tenderness, swelling/bruising
- Shock

Treatment
- Keep immobilised where the casualty is lying
- Keep steady until splinted/gentle traction
- Support in the most comfortable position
- Dress open fractures before splinting
- Don't miss other less obvious conditions
- Treat for shock

Burns

Symptoms are:
- Severe pain at the site of injury, numbness if a deep burn
- Sometimes blistering, grey, charred, peeling skin
- Shock

Treatment
- Reassure casualty and cool affected area
- Remove constrictions and protect affected area
- DO NOT break blisters or apply lotions or adhesive dressings
- Treat for shock

Dislocations

Symptoms are
- Pain, limited or no articulation of joint
- Deformity or abnormal appearance, swelling and bruising

Treatment
- Support and keep limb steady in most comfortable position.
- DO NOT attempt to reset ☐

Appendix four – BSAC history

The British Sub-Aqua Club – a brief history

The British Sub-Aqua Club (BSAC) was founded in London in 1953 by a small number of pioneers of diving in the UK. Their declared aim was 'to promote underwater exploration, science and safety'. Within a year this group numbered more than 100 and was officially recognised as the governing body for the then new sport of underwater swimming. By January 1955 the BSAC had more than 1,100 members and had established its enduring branch system, forming branches around the United Kingdom and overseas.

Already international in nature, in 1959 the BSAC was a founding member of the World Underwater Federation, CMAS. In 1959 the first BSAC *Diving Manual* was published, the forerunner of what was destined to become a bestselling and highly respected range of diver training books and support materials. With its membership approaching 7,000, in 1965 the BSAC started recording and analysing all UK recreational diving incidents, publicly reporting its findings in order to improve diving safety. This continues today with the annual publication of the much acclaimed BSAC Incidents Report, covering all UK sport diving incidents. The UK's adoption of the metric system in 1972 was also marked by the publication of a metric version of the Royal Navy decompression tables, specially designed for the BSAC. This table was the forerunner of the BSAC '88 Decompression Tables, which in turn were the first to be totally designed for recreational diving. They cover sea level and altitude diving, and have been expanded to cover nitrox diving.

Responding to the expansion of the recreational diving market, in 1976 the BSAC launched its schools system. BSAC-recognised schools are independent businesses using BSAC-certified instructors to deliver the BSAC diver-training programme and award BSAC qualifications. The BSAC celebrated its 25th Anniversary with a banquet at the Mansion House in London together with its new President, HRH the Prince of Wales.

As the club continued to grow, reaching more than 30,000 members in 1979, it was re-organised as a company limited by guarantee. The removal of administrative financial support following changes in government policy meant the BSAC had to seek additional income streams. The range of manuals was increased and other opportunities to realise the value of the BSAC's unique experience and knowledge were explored. In 1987 a wholly owned subsidiary company, BSAC International, was created and a contract signed with a major Japanese trading company to create BSAC Japan. The ensuing income has allowed the BSAC to survive and continue to grow, as BSAC Japan has developed into a major and respected player in the more commercial Japanese diving market. It has also served as a model for other international operations including the development of BSAC Korea.

After many years of co-habitation with the British Sports Council at various London addresses, BSAC relocated its headquarters in 1990 to its own new waterside office complex in Ellesmere Port, Cheshire.

At its 40th Anniversary celebration banquet in the historic London Guildhall, HRH The Prince of Wales, BSAC President, presented the club with its own coat of arms. During the 1990s the BSAC continued to develop and modernise its training programme, introducing the Ocean Diver entry-level course and a wide range of student and instructor support materials. To maintain and develop its overseas branches, schools and franchises without encumbrance, the BSAC separated from CMAS and strengthened its ties with the European Underwater Federation (EUF). Joining the Internet revolution the BSAC launched its own website in 1996 at www.bsac.com – a project which now offers online information, product sales and course bookings and has seen more than 10,000,000 hits annually.

In keeping with its long history of protecting British divers' interests in the development of European Standards for diving equipment, the BSAC has also played a leading role in the development of European Standards for diving services, covering diver training instructors and dive centres.

With some 45,000 members registered through the UK HQ, the BSAC is the world's largest diving club besides being the oldest and one of the most respected international diver training agencies. Its policy of continuous development and improvement ensures it is at the forefront of safe yet adventurous diving and diver training.

Those interested in joining the BSAC can obtain details at www.bsac.org □

BSAC organisation

In most countries around the world, the national recreational-diving federations are comprised of numerous independent diving clubs, creating a hierarchical structure where control is vested in club presidents rather than individual divers. BSAC has a unique 'flat' structure where individual divers are full members of the club, either as direct members or through membership of a BSAC branch. All full members possess equal voting rights and have equal rights of election to the BSAC Council, with the exception of two positions, those of the Honorary Treasurer and the National Diving Officer, which require additional technical qualification.

Branches reflect this structure, being largely autonomous organisations made up of BSAC members following model constitutions approved by the parent club and are run by an elected committee. In order to train divers, branches must use instructors who hold BSAC-issued qualifications and follow the current BSAC training programme.

Initially, diving in Britain developed through the ability of branches to provide the infrastructure needed by divers – access to swimming pools for training, compressors for cylinder filling, boats for dive site access – coupled with the knowledge and expertise required to learn and develop diving skills. In addition to this, most branches also offer an enjoyable social aspect to diving and the attraction that because the instructors, though fully qualified, are unpaid volunteers training is inexpensive.

Today, entry-level diver training can also be obtained through a number of commercial diving schools, many of which use BSAC-qualified instructors to deliver BSAC training. These schools can more easily offer training tailored to suit a busy customer's requirements when time is at a premium. Of course, schools are independent commercial entities and have to charge commercial rates in order to survive. To enhance their service, some schools also offer more advanced training, often including diving in more exotic waters as part of the package.

Most branches, as well as offering training, have a comprehensive diving programme organised by the branch committee, using either branch-owned boats or hired vessels. Some of these activities are week-long expeditions, possibly using chartered liveaboards, or organised trips to overseas dive

locations. Many such trips are arranged as family activities, making diving more accessible both socially and economically for those with families, and enabling partners and even children to participate. Note that BSAC schools have a minimum age of 12 years for scuba use and branches have a minimum age of 14 years, though some branches set a higher limit or require immediate parental supervision. Some special branches draw members from limited social groups such as universities, companies or the military, and these branches may not be able to accept the general public as members.

The wide range of branch diving makes it the ideal way to broaden and develop diving experience, and the full range of services offered by BSAC is available to members. On offer is a wide range of skill development courses (SDCs), some of these branch-run and some organised at regional level by the BSAC Coaching Scheme. Because of the extensive range of advanced training events offered by BSAC, and the unique opportunities for gaining experience in its branches, many divers and instructors trained by other agencies join the club to develop their diving. Such divers are welcomed by branches or can join BSAC directly with full recognition of their previous training and experience. Many SDCs are also open to non-members and can be booked at www.bsac.org. □

Appendix six– Qualifications

BSAC diver qualifications

BSAC First Class Diver

This grade demands a higher than average level of theoretical knowledge and organisational and personal diving skills. First Class Divers have a broad range of practical experience and are capable of planning, organising and leading advanced level diving expeditions. This grade is awarded following a nationally conducted assessment.

BSAC Advanced Divers

This grade requires that divers have considerable diving experience and have developed their skills to a level that enables them to competently organise and lead diving expeditions. They will have additional experience in managing diving in a wide range of conditions and circumstances.

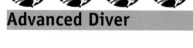

BSAC Dive Leaders

To reach this level divers will require considerable dive management and rescue management skills and be competent in organising and leading diving groups. Their dive planning, conduct and navigational abilities will qualify them to act as dive guides. This grade meets and exceeds the proposed European Level 3 diver standard.

BSAC Sports Divers

At this level, divers may dive autonomously to a depth of 35m in waters that match their previous training and experience. They can also conduct dives requiring in-water decompression and are trained in more comprehensive rescue skills, including basic surface resuscitation.

BSAC Ocean Divers

This grade allows divers to dive autonomously with others of the same or higher grades. Divers are trained to elementary buddy rescue level. Dives are limited to a depth of 20m operating in waters similar to those they have trained in. Ocean Divers are not trained to conduct dives requiring in-water decompression stops or to dive without more experienced surface support. This grade meets and exceeds the proposed European Level 2 diver standard.

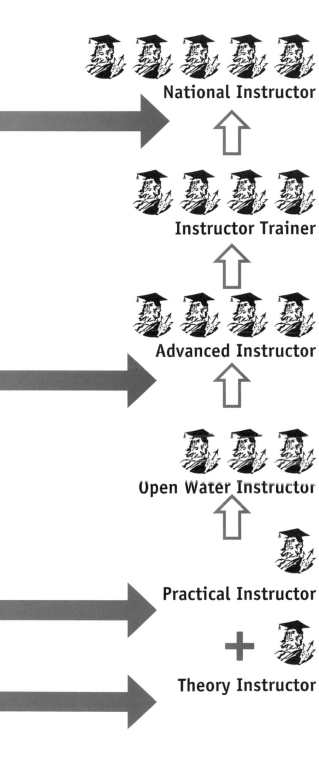

National Instructor

Instructor Trainer

Advanced Instructor

Open Water Instructor

Practical Instructor

+

Theory Instructor

BSAC instructor qualifications

BSAC National Instructor

To gain this qualification, the highest BSAC instructor grade, the candidate must have previously qualified as a BSAC First Class Diver. National Instructors are used in the training and assessment of other instructors and as team leaders in the BSAC Instructor Training Scheme.

BSAC Instructor Trainer

A BSAC Advanced Instructor who has received further instruction and assessment enabling him or her to participate in the BSAC Instructor Training Scheme as a trainer of other instructors.

BSAC Advanced Instructor

A BSAC Open Water Instructor with considerable diving and instructional experience who has received further training and assessment. Advanced Instructors are qualified to teach a wide range of skills and to supervise the work of other instructors.

BSAC Open Water Instructor

A BSAC instructor who is qualified to teach both theoretical and practical diving in classrooms, and in both sheltered and open-water environments.

BSAC Practical Instructor

A BSAC instructor who has received training in practical instructional techniques and limited assessment which allows him or her to provide instruction in practical diving skills.

BSAC Theory Instructor

A BSAC instructor who has received training in instructional techniques and theory assessment which allows him or her to provide instruction in diving theory subjects. □

Note: All BSAC instructors are trained and assessed through the nationally organised BSAC Instructor Training Scheme.

Minimum diver level required in order to take instructor qualification

Appendix seven – Code of Conduct

Divers' Code of Conduct

The BSAC Divers' Code of Conduct is designed to encourage good behaviour at dive sites and when diving, and to ensure that divers do not come into conflict with other water users.

Dive planning

Contact the nearest BSAC branch or dive school local to the dive site for advice on local conditions and regulations.

At the dive site

- Obtain permission before diving in restricted areas, such as harbours, estuaries or private waters.
- Thank all the relevant parties before you leave and ensure any dues are paid.
- Avoid overcrowding sites and show consideration to other users.
- Park sensibly, avoiding obstruction and damage to verges. Use proper car parks and pay parking fees.
- Keep launching ramps and slipways clear and be economical with use of space.
- Keep the peace, do not operate compressors or boat and car engines unsociably.
- Do not litter. Close gates. Be careful about fires. Avoid any damage to land or crops.
- Obey special instructions such as National Trust rules, local bylaws and regulations about camping and caravanning.
- Remember, our equipment makes divers conspicuous and bad behaviour can result in future restrictions.

In and on the water

- Make your boats identifiable, this can help rescue agencies and shows you have nothing to hide.
- Seek advice about, and permission for, launching and follow it.
- Inform the coastguard or a responsible person of your operational plan and report when your diving is complete.
- Avoid diving near buoys, pots and pot markers.
- Ask local fishermen where it is advisable *not* to dive.
- Avoid disturbing local wildlife such as sea bird or seal colonies.

- Avoid diving in fairways or areas of heavy surface traffic and observe the International Regulations for Preventing Collisions at Sea. Commercial traffic usually has restricted manoeuvring capability.
- Always fly the diving flag when conducting diving operations, but not when the boat is in transit. Do not leave boats unattended.
- Do not come in to bathing beaches under power, do use any special approach lanes and avoid creating unnecessary wash in restricted waterways or moorings.
- Use surface marker buoys where appropriate.
- Respect local bylaws, regulations and customs.

On conservation

- Do not use a spear-gun when scuba diving.
- Collecting marine creatures of any kind is damaging to the environment and often subject to legal control. Take photographs and notes, not specimens.

On wrecks

- Do not dive on a designated, protected wreck site without specific authority. These are generally indicated on charts and marked by buoys or warning notices on the shore nearby.
- Do not disturb anything that appears to be of historical importance.
- If you discover a wreck, do not disturb anything and report its position and any other details to the relevant authorities.
- Be aware that many wrecks involved loss of life and as such can be sensitive areas and deserve respect.
- Follow the BSAC wreck policy – look, don't touch: more detailed advice on wreck diving is published on the BSAC website: www.bsac.org

Diving freedoms stem from responsible diving, it is up to us as divers to behave sensibly and sociably – and keep to the Divers' Code. □

Index

Index

Index

Photographs

Bob Brading:

pages 17, top left, bottom right; 18; 19; 20; 21; 30; 36; 37; 38; 39; 40; 41; 42; 43; 48, right; 50; 51; 54, left; 57, right; 59; 66; 68; 69; 72; 84, right; 85; 87; 96; 100; 103; 104; 105; 106; 107; 108; 109; 114; 115; 116; 117; 124; 126; 127; 131, worm, nudibranch and ray; 133, right; 134, right; 138; 139, left; 140; 141; 142; 143.

Julian Calverley:

cover; chapter breaks, pages 14; 22; 32; 52; 60; 74; 98; 118; 128; 156; 159.

***DIVE* magazine:**

pages 31, right; 45; 70; 77; 78; 79; 81; 125; 133, left; 134, left.

Charles Hood:

pages 17, except top left and bottom right; 25; 27; 29; 31, left; 44; 47; 48, left; 54, right; 55; 56, left; 57, left; 58; 67; 80; 84, left; 88; 89; 90; 92; 93; 95; 101; 102; 112; 120; 122; 123; 130; 131, except nudibranch, worm and ray; 132; 136; 137; 139, right.

Gavin Newman:

page 135.

Simon Rogerson:

pages 73; 110.

Douglas David Seifert:

page 56, right.

Suunto:

page 76.

The British Sub-Aqua Club gratefully acknowledges the assistance provided by numerous members, schools, and friends in the diving trade in the development of this book.

Cover photograph by Julian Calverley,

website: www.calverley.co.uk